Math Activities for Young Children

A Resource Guide for Parents and Teachers

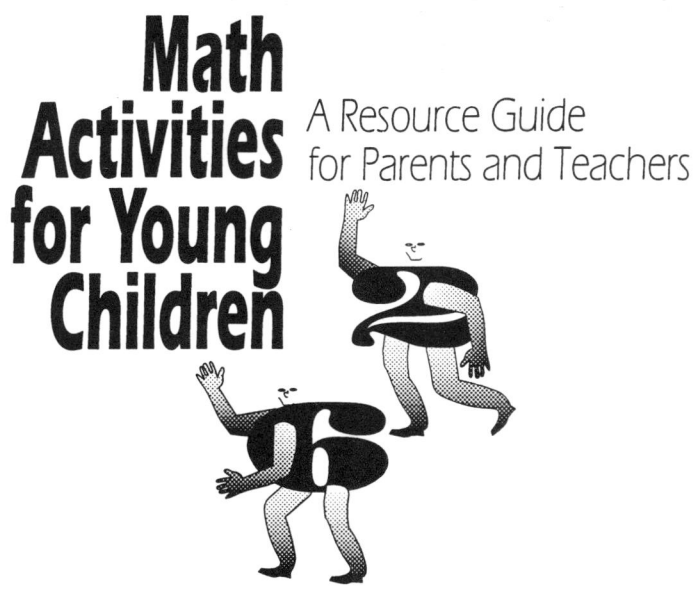

Robert J. Gamble
Julia Wilkins
D'Youville College

McGraw-Hill, Inc.
College Custom Series

New York St. Louis San Francisco Auckland Bogotá
Caracas Lisbon London Madrid Mexico Milan Montreal
New Delhi Paris San Juan Singapore Sydney Tokyo Toronto

McGraw-Hill's College Custom Series consists of products that are produced from camera-ready copy. Peer review, class testing, and accuracy are primarily the responsibility of the author(s).

Math Activities for Young Children
A Resource Guide for Parents and Teachers

Copyright © 1995 by McGraw-Hill, Inc. All rights reserved. Printed in the United States of America. Except as permitted under the United States Copyright Act of 1976, no part of this publication may be reproduced or distributed in any form or by any means, or stored in a data base retrieval system, without prior written permission of the publisher.

   2 3 4 5 6 7 8 9 0 HAM HAM 9 0 9 8 7 6

ISBN 0-07-022812-4

Editor: Reaney Dorsey

Cover Design: Maggie Lytle

Printer/Binder: HAMCO/NETPUB Corporation

About the Authors

Robert Gamble is an Assistant Professor at D'Youville College in Buffalo, N.Y. He has a Ph.D. from The State University of New York at Buffalo in Early Childhood Education and is a former preschool director and elementary school teacher.

Julia Wilkins holds a Master's Degree from the University of Bristol, England, and has a publishing diploma from The London College of Printing. She obtained her New York State Teacher's Certification from D'Youville College in Buffalo, N.Y.

About the Illustrator

Robert Sabatini has a bachelor's degree from the University of Toronto and a Teacher's Certificate in Elementary Education from D'Youville College in Buffalo, N.Y.

Acknowledgments

We would like to thank the D'Youville College education students who provided suggestions and ideas for this book, Betty C. Gamble, for her editorial skills, and Dr. Robert DiSibio for supporting this project.

Contents

SECTION I
Matching Activities   1
Sequencing Numbers   39
Sorting and Classifying   57
Working with Shapes   77

SECTION II
Adding Skills   99
Subtracting Skills   137

SECTION III
Using Money   165
Telling Time   197

Introduction

This book has been written for parents and teachers who would like children to value mathematics and experience the excitement of discovery. In today's society, people increasingly need the ability to think logically, reason, communicate, and solve problems. By working through the activities in this book, you can help your child achieve these goals by introducing her to some basic math concepts. These concepts will form the foundation for later higher level understanding.

The activities have been designed to motivate and encourage initiative through active exploration with familiar objects. All recommended materials are inexpensive, recyclable, and easily accessible. Only food products that will be consumed are used.

The recommended materials are listed at the beginning of each chapter. However, these materials can be easily substituted for any materials you consider appropriate. The activities have been designed to allow for flexibility and can be easily modified or elaborated upon depending upon the abilities of your child.

All activities are noncompetitive and most can be carried out individually or in small groups. When the participation of more than one child is necessary, it is stated under the title.

The activities throughout the book progress from easy to more complex, with a continuous emphasis on developing prerequisite skills and knowledge that will provide a foundation for future mathematical concept development. It is recommended that your child "master" the skills in one chapter before progressing to the next, but it is not important that your child attempt every activity in this book. Rather, it is suggested that you use it as a resource guide over a period of years. Your child may grasp the concepts in "Sorting and Classifying", but not be ready for "Telling Time", so it is suggested that you shelve the book for a period time.

Alternately, your child may have already acquired the skills necessary for activities in the early chapters, in which case you may wish to begin with more complex activities introduced later on.

The female pronoun is used throughout in an attempt to overcome the negative messages that discourage girls from math.

Section I

Matching Activities

The activities in this chapter help to increase the child's understanding that numerals represent quantity and therefore have both intangible and object meaning. In this way, the child comes to realize that numbers can be represented and used in many different ways.

At the beginning of the chapter, the child is introduced to basic counting, and as the chapter progresses, she learns to apply this knowledge in a variety of fashions. Number recognition, counting skills, and writing skills are continually reinforced throughout the activities.

These matching activities provide the foundation for understanding higher order mathematical thinking. It is therefore suggested that the concepts introduced in this chapter be "mastered" before progressing to the next chapter.

Recommended Materials

Barrettes
Small box
Construction paper
Egg carton
Glue
Gold stars
Index cards
Jars or plastic containers
Marker
Newspaper
Pennies
Pens
Plain paper
Large plastic ball
Plastic eggs or ping pong balls
Poster board
Scissors
Tag board
Small wooden beads
Wool or yarn

6   *Matching Activities*

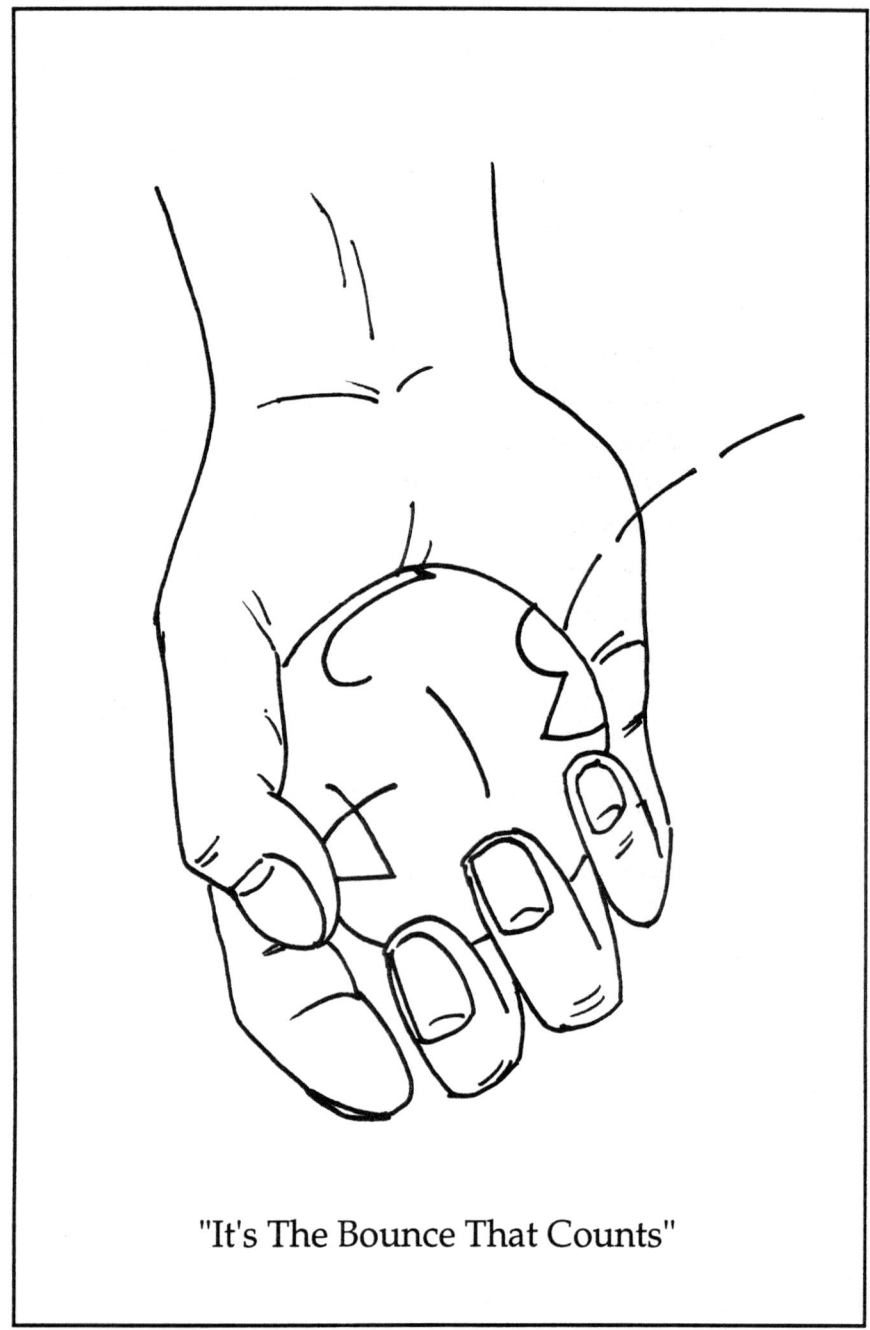

"It's The Bounce That Counts"

"It's The Bounce That Counts"

Objectives
To promote:
~ number recognition
~ counting skills
~ development of small motor skills

Materials
* Large plastic ball
* Marker

Activity
Mark numbers 1 to 10 on different parts of the ball. Throw ball to the child. She will look at the numeral under her right thumb, say it out loud, and bounce the ball the corresponding number of times.

8   *Matching Activities*

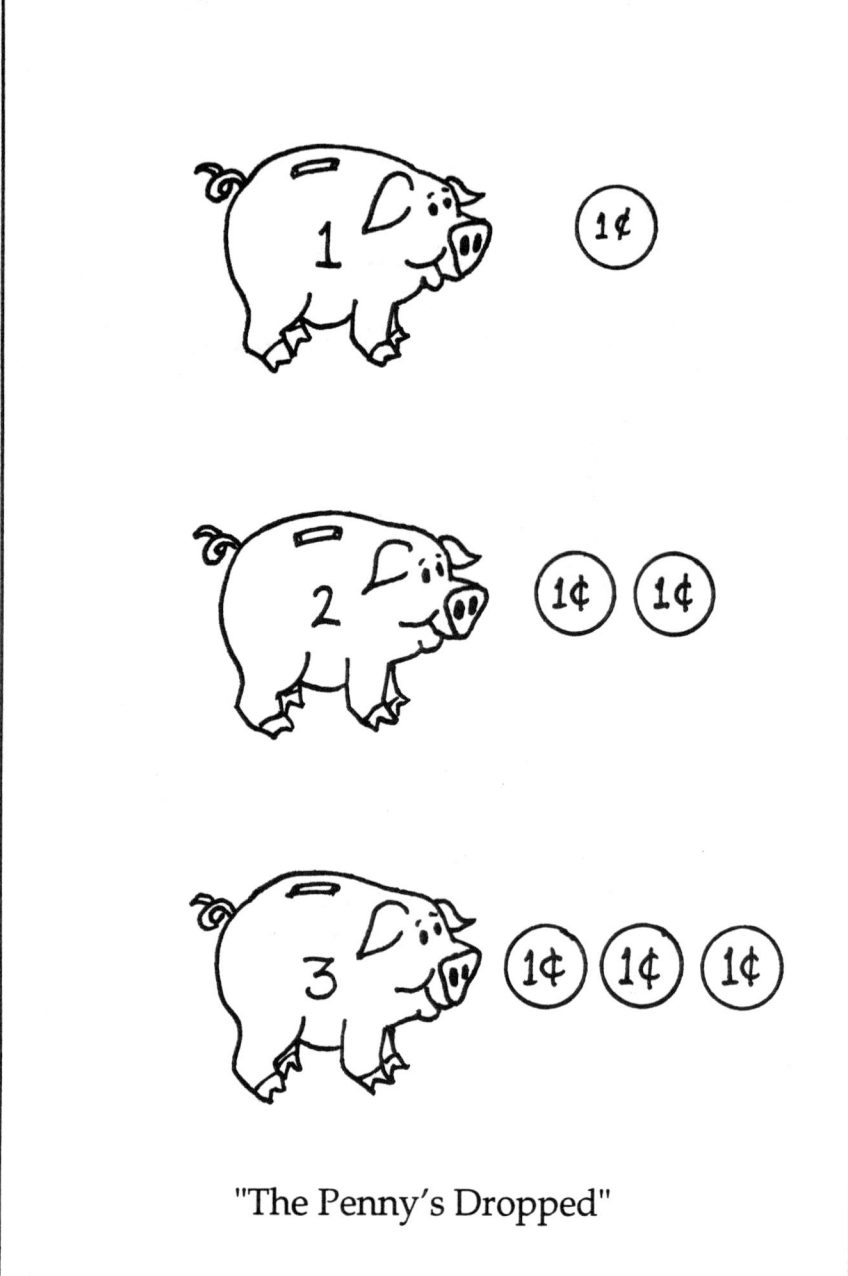

"The Penny's Dropped"

"The Penny's Dropped"

Objectives

To promote: ~ number correspondence
~ counting skills
~ development of small motor skills

Materials

* Ten piggy banks (jars or plastic containers can be used)
* Marker
* Fifty-five pennies

Activity

Number "piggy banks" 1 to 10. Give child fifty-five pennies. She will then drop the correct number of pennies into each piggy bank.

10　*Matching Activities*

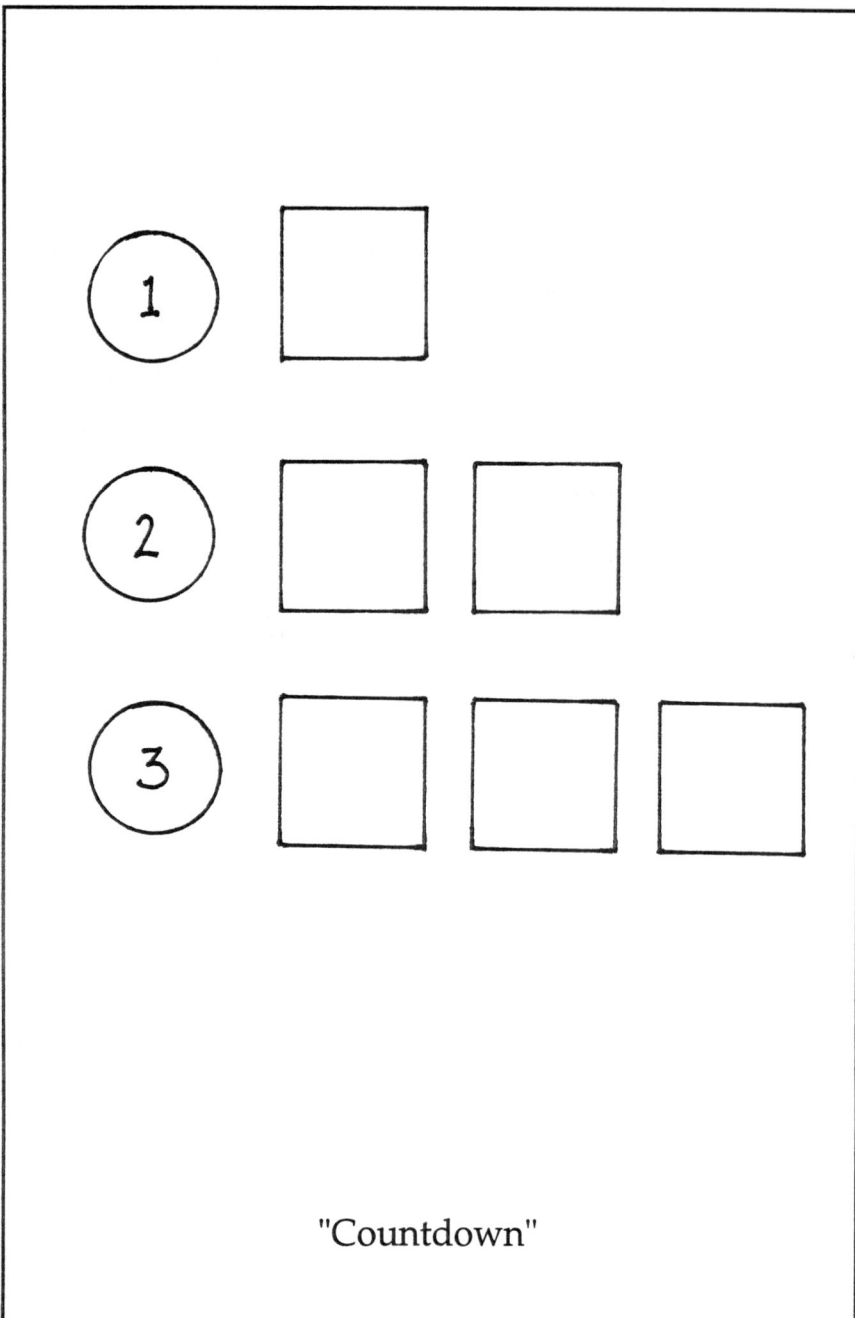

"Countdown"

Objectives

To promote:
~ counting skills
~ matching skills
~ number recognition

Materials

* Ten 3-inch circles of tag board, numbered 1 to 10
* Fifty-five 2-inch squares of colorful construction paper
* Small box
* Scissors
* Marker

Activity

Place numbered pieces of tag board in small box. Child will remove circles from box and place them in numerical order in a vertical line. She will then place the appropriate number of squares beside each circle to match the number shown.

12 *Matching Activities*

"Claire's Hair"

"Claire's Hair"

Objectives

To promote: ~ number identification
~ visual perception
~ development of small motor skills

Materials

* Large face (can be drawn on construction paper)
* Wool or yarn
* Twenty-one barrettes
* Markers
* Glue

Activity

From wool or yarn make six braids and glue them around the face. Print numerals 1 to 6 underneath each one. Child will attach the corresponding number of barrettes to each braid.

14 *Matching Activities*

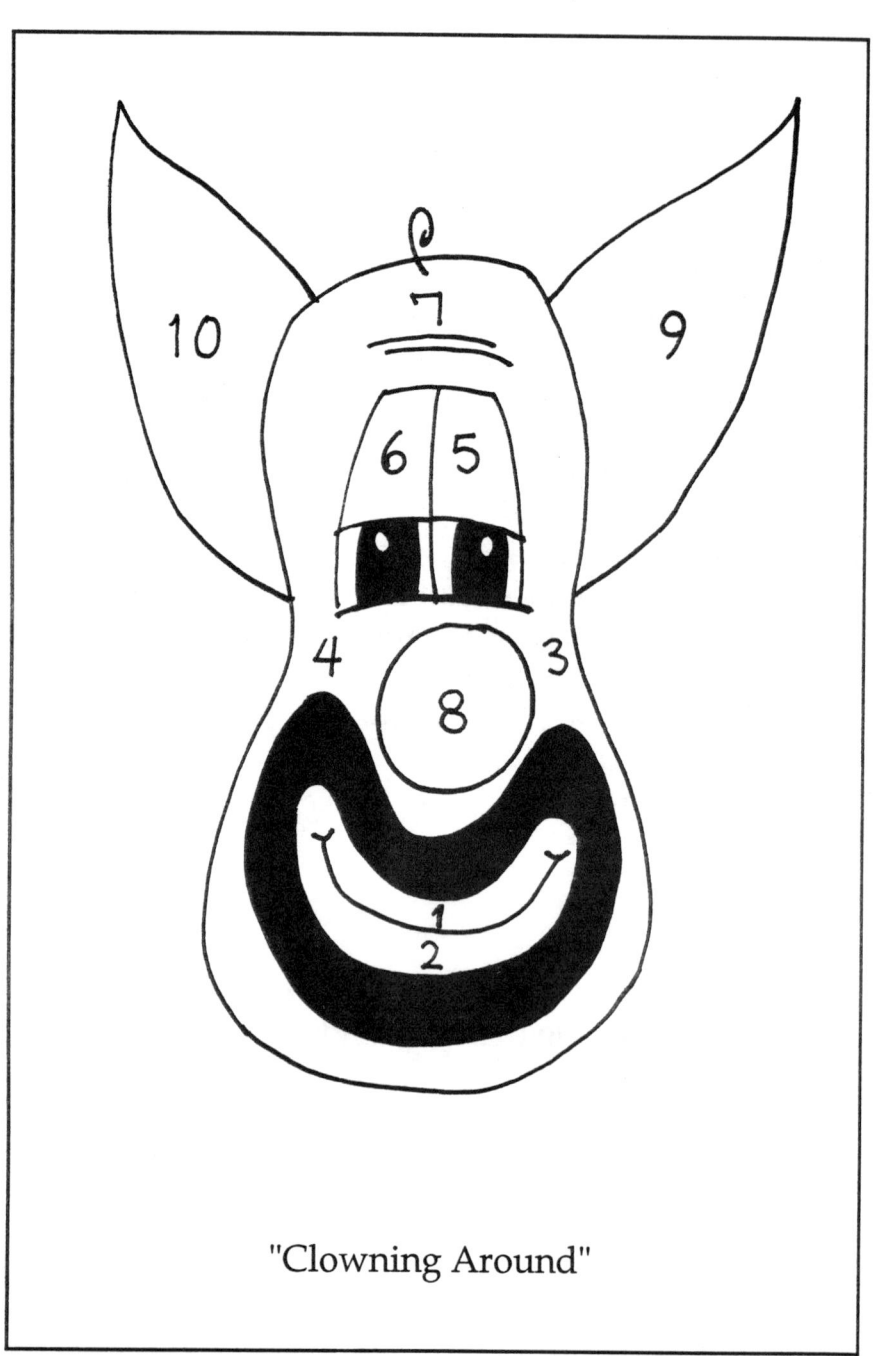

"Clowning Around"

"Clowning Around"

Objectives
To promote: ~ matching skills
~ number identification
~ manipulative skills

Materials
* Clown's face (can be drawn on poster board)
* Large gold stars
* Marker

Activity
Print numerals 1 to 10 on different parts of the clown's face. Give child fifty-five gold stars. She will then cover the numerals on the face with the corresponding number of stars.

16 *Matching Activities*

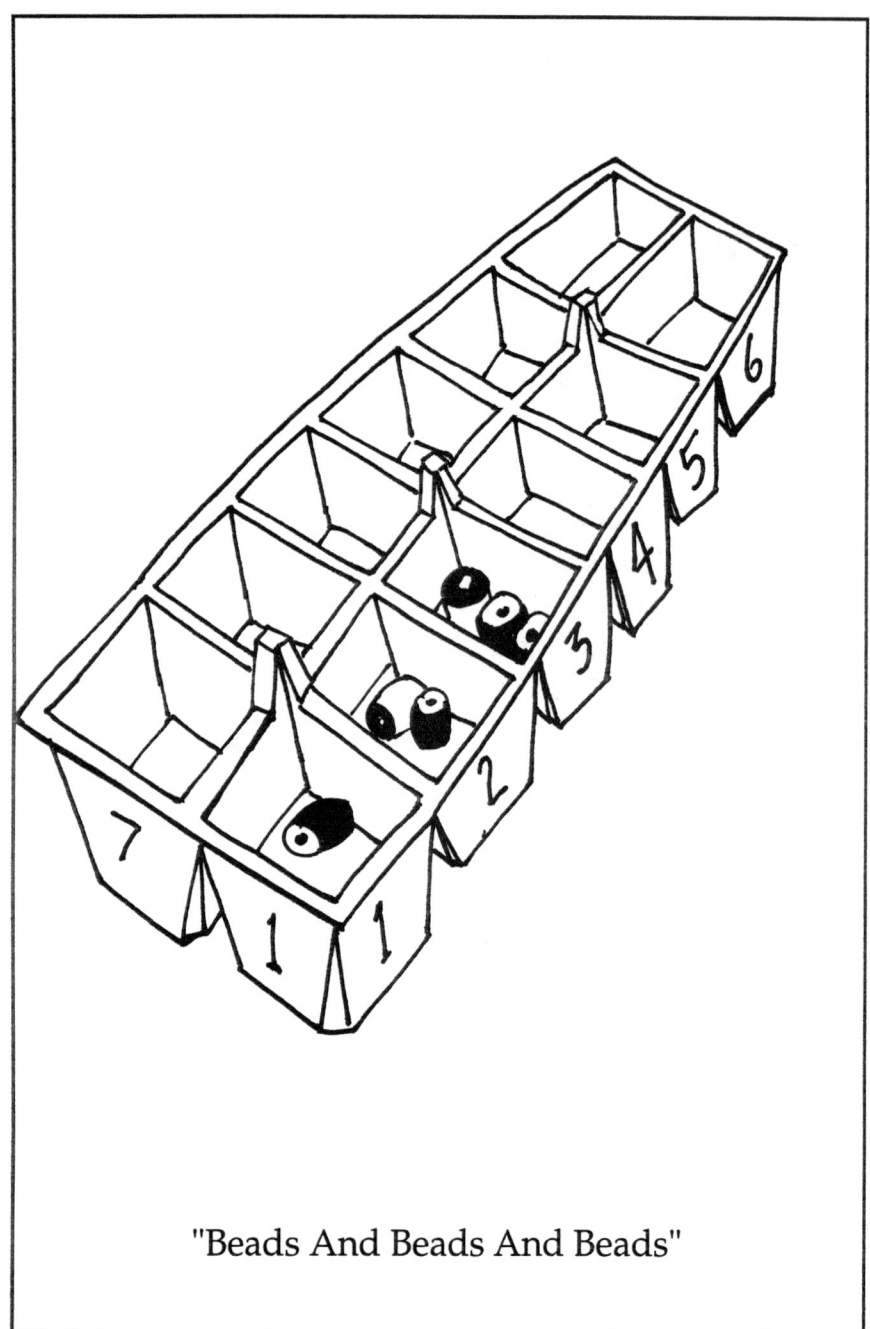

"Beads And Beads And Beads"

"Beads And Beads And Beads"

Objectives
To promote: ~ counting skills
~ number recognition
~ manipulative skills

Materials
* Small wooden beads
* Egg carton

Activity
Print numerals 1 to 12 on cups of the egg carton. Child will place the corresponding number of beads in each cup.

18   *Matching Activities*

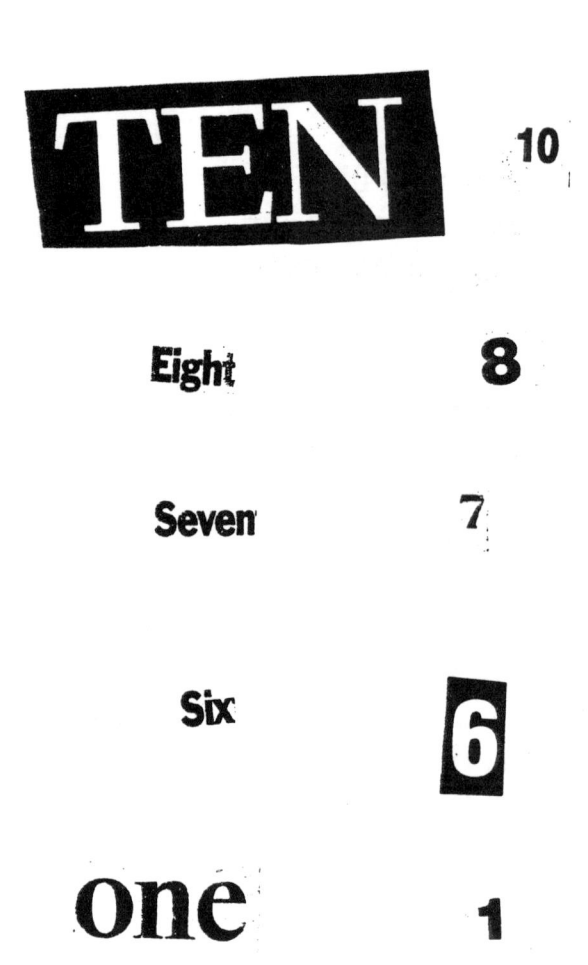

TEN   10

Eight   8

Seven   7

Six   **6**

one   1

"Number Two - Where Are You?"

"Number Two - Where Are You?"

Objectives
To promote: ~ one to one correspondence
~ manipulative skills
~ visual perception

Materials
* Newspaper
* Sheet of paper
* Scissors
* Glue

Activity
Child will cut out five numbers written in words from the newspaper. She will then look through the paper to find the corresponding printed numeral for each word. The words and numerals can then be stuck next to each other on a plain sheet of paper.

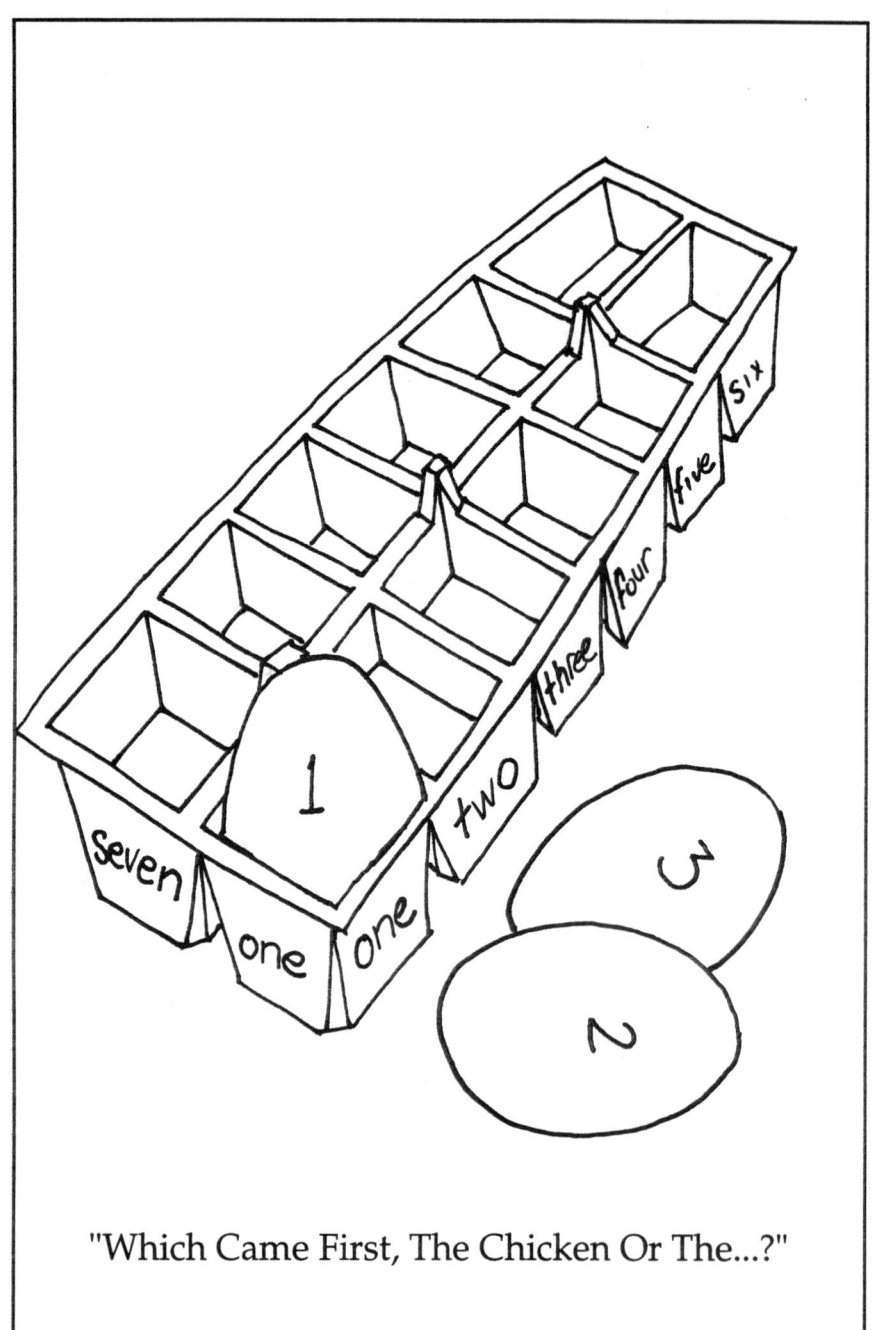

"Which Came First, The Chicken Or The...?"

Objectives
To promote: ~ matching skills
~ number recognition
~ development of small motor skills

Materials
* Twelve plastic eggs (ping pong balls can be used)
* Egg carton
* Marker

Activity
Number the first egg with the numeral "1", the second egg with the numeral "2", etc. Then write the written words "one" to "twelve" on each cup of the egg carton. Child will place each egg in the cup of the egg carton with the corresponding number.

22 *Matching Activities*

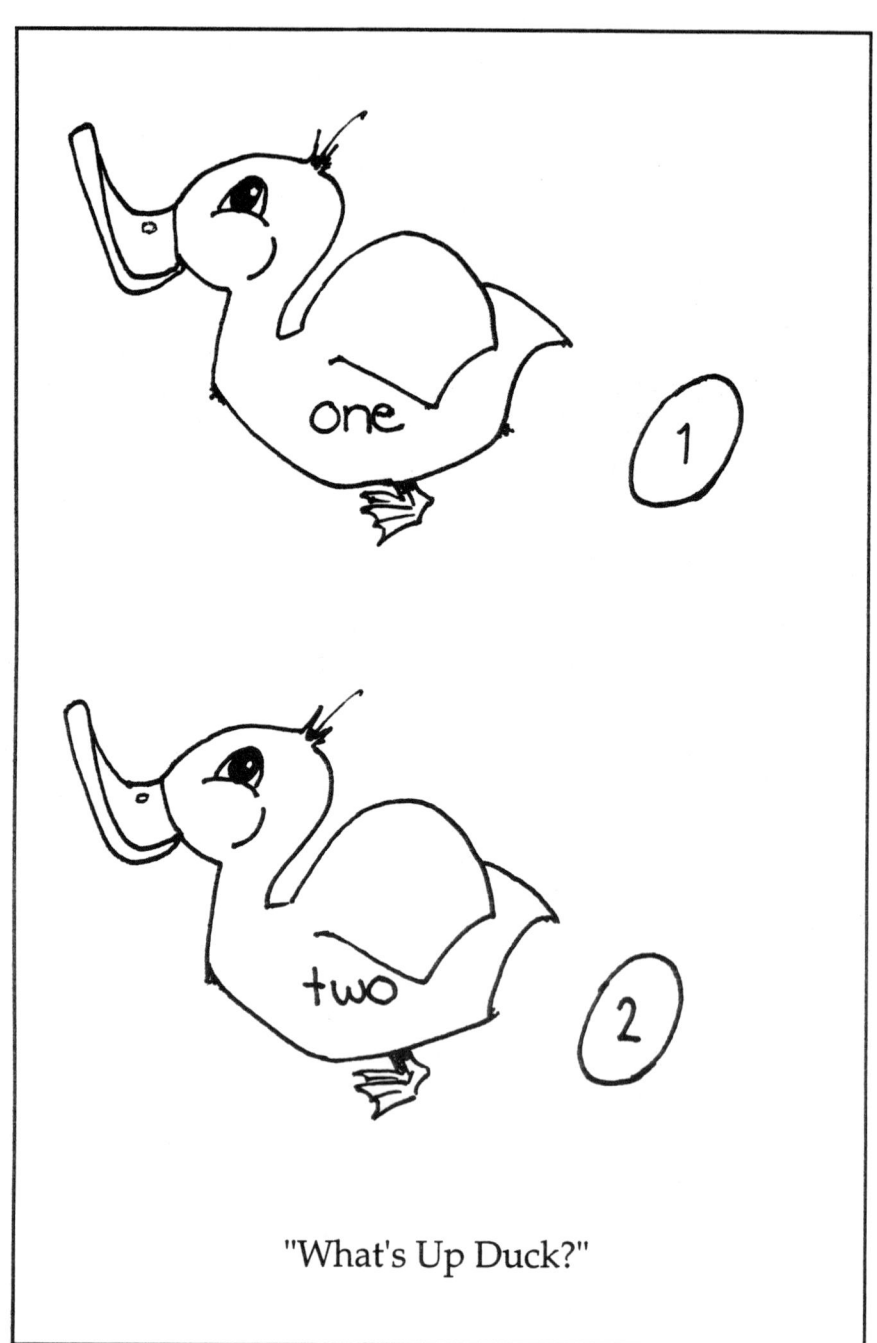

"What's Up Duck?"

Objectives
To promote: ~ matching skills
~ number correspondence
~ visual perception

Materials
* White and green construction paper
* Markers
* Scissors
* Glue

Activity

From green construction paper, cut out fifteen large ducks and mark the first one with the word "one", the second one with the word "two", etc. Then cut out fifteen egg shapes from white construction paper, and mark them with numerals 1 to 15. Child will match the eggs to the ducks with the corresponding numerals.

24   *Matching Activities*

1) one ☐

2) two ☐ ☐

3) three ☐ ☐ ☐

"My Word!"

"My Word!"

Objectives

To promote:
~ counting skills
~ number correspondence
~ visual discrimination

Materials

* Ten 3-inch circles of tag board, numbered 1 to 10
* Ten pieces of tag board, marked with the words "one" to "ten"
* Fifty-five 2-inch squares of colorful construction paper
* Small box   * Scissors   * Marker

Activity

Place the numerals and written words in a small box. Child will remove the numerals from the box and place them in numerical order in a vertical line. Next to each numeral she will place the corresponding written word, and then the number of squares to match each numeral.

26   *Matching Activities*

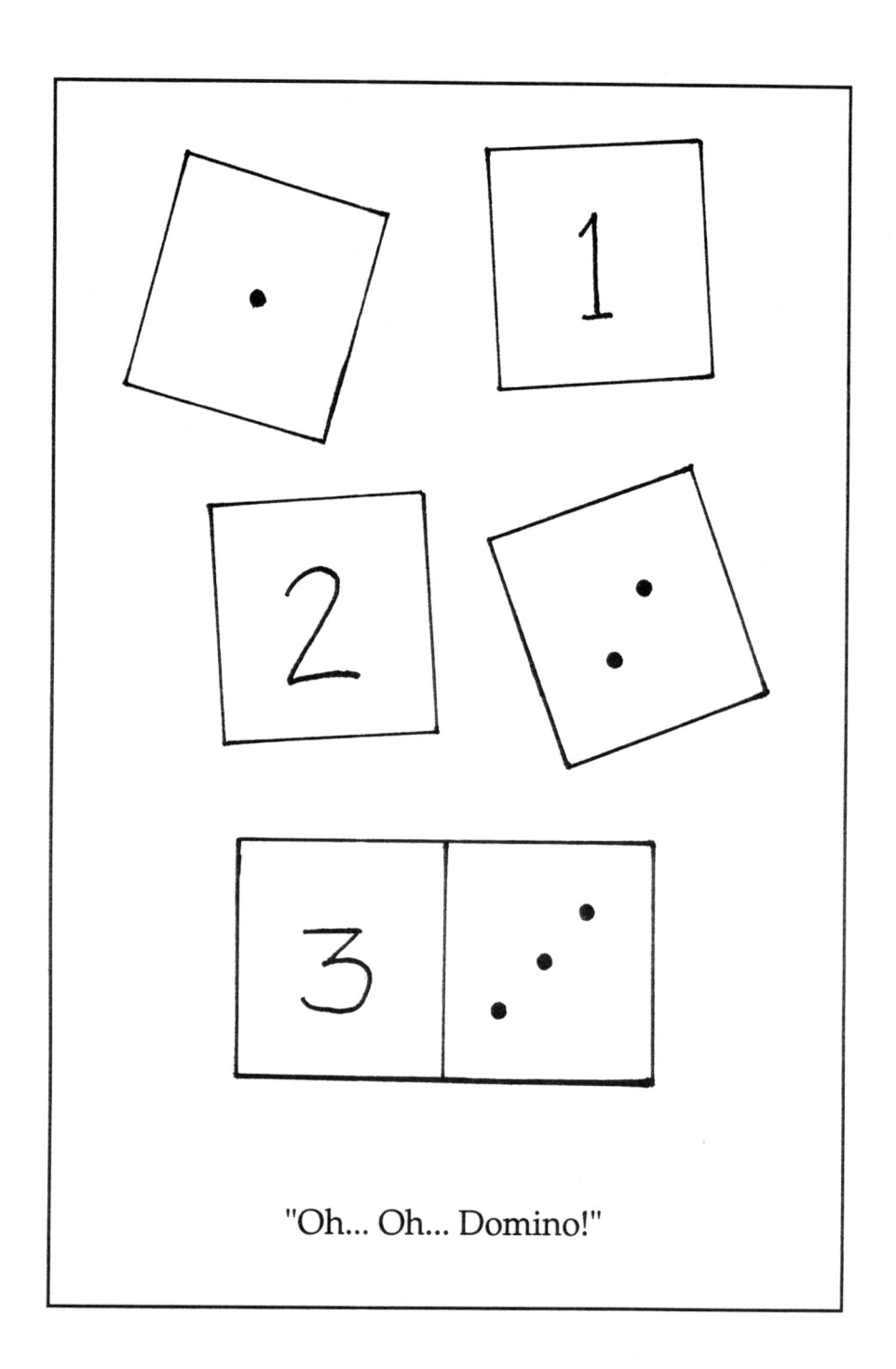

"Oh... Oh... Domino!"

"Oh... Oh... Domino!"

Objectives

To promote: ~ matching skills
~ number recognition
~ development of small motor skills
~ eye-hand coordination

Materials

* Poster board
* Marker
* Scissors

Activity

From posterboard cut out twenty rectangles. Write on half of each rectangle, printing the numeral "1" on the first one, "2" on the second one, etc. Use the remaining space to draw the corresponding number of dots. Cut each rectangle in half so that the numerals and dots are separated. Spread numerals and dots over table. Child will make dominos by correctly matching them together.

28   *Matching Activities*

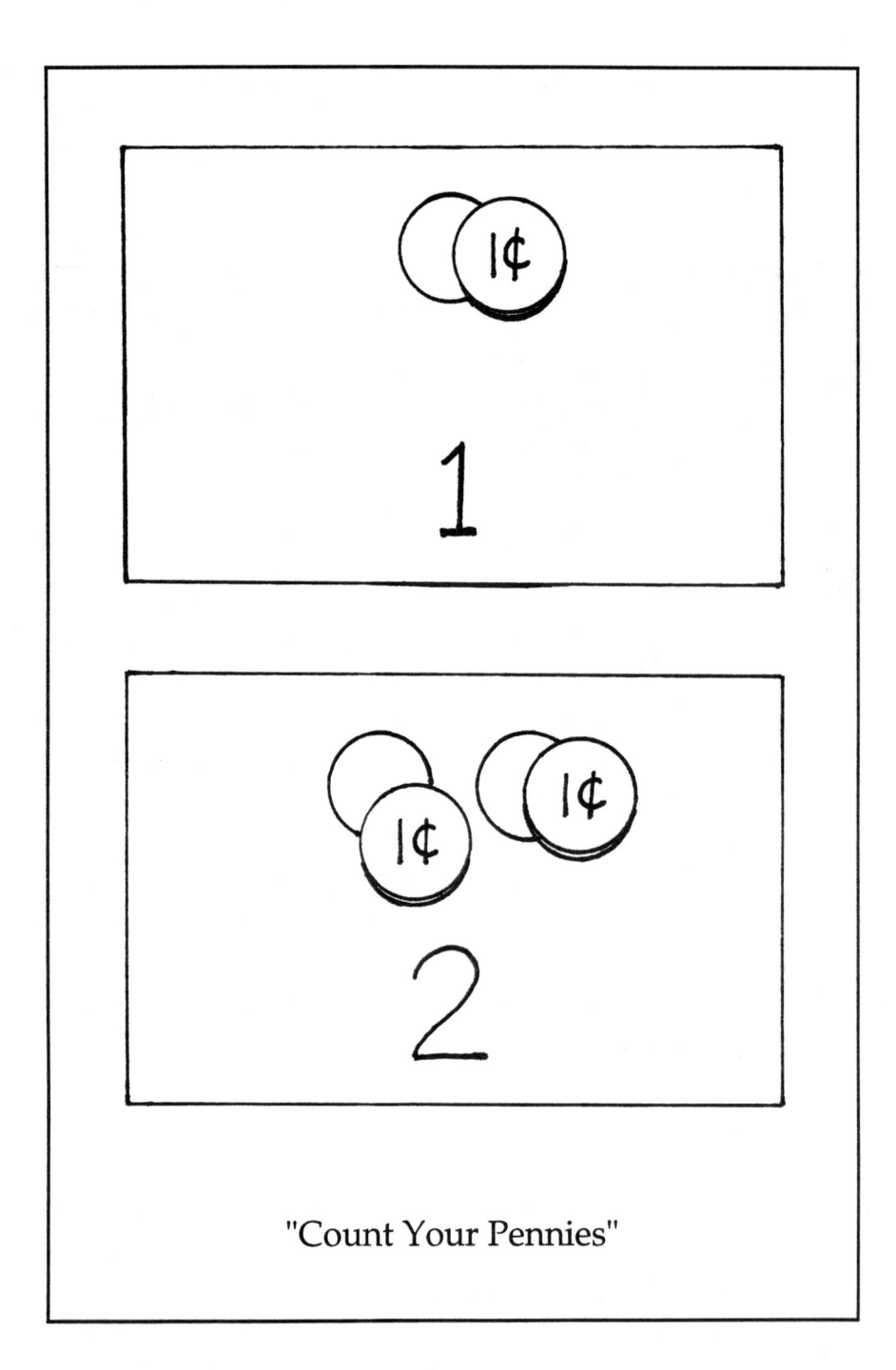

1

2

"Count Your Pennies"

"Count Your Pennies"

Objectives

To promote: ~ matching skills
~ counting skills
~ eye-hand coordination
~ writing skills

Materials

* Ten 3 x 5 index cards
* Fifty-five pennies
* Pencil

Activity

Trace one penny on the first card, two pennies on the second card, etc. Give child fifty-five pennies. She will place each penny on a circle, then write the corresponding numeral at the bottom of each card.

30   *Matching Activities*

"The Stars Are Out"

"The Stars Are Out"

Objectives
To promote: ~ counting skills
~ number correspondence
~ writing skills

Materials
* Large cardboard cut-outs of numerals 1 to 10
* Large size ready-stick stars
* Scissors
* Pen

Activity
Display numerals 1 to 10 at the front of the room. Child will stick the corresponding number of stars on each numeral, then write the correct number in words below the stars.

1 2 3 4 5 6 7 8 9 10
one

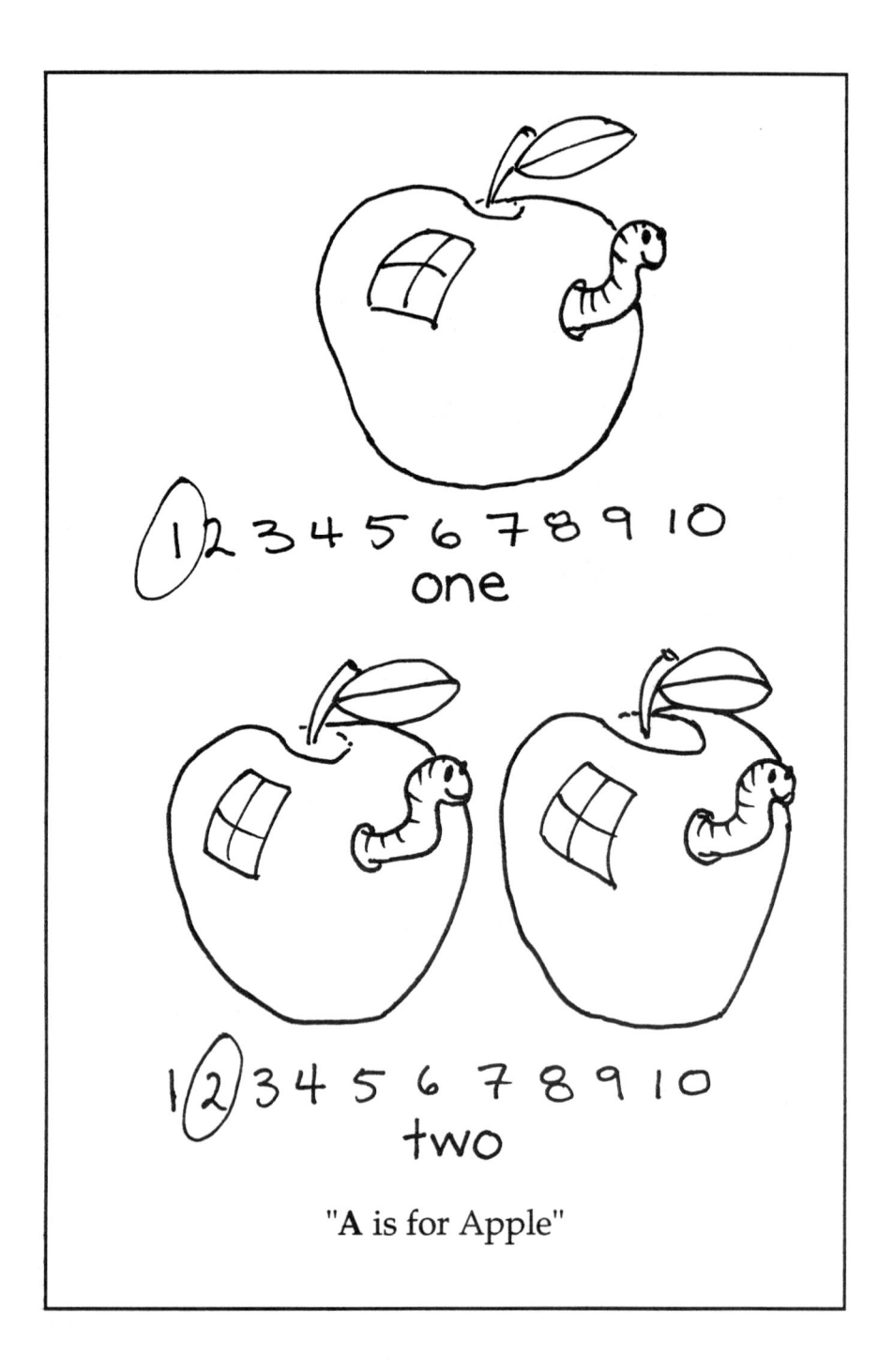

1 2 3 4 5 6 7 8 9 10
two

"**A** is for Apple"

"A is for Apple"

Objectives
To promote: ~ counting skills
~ number identification
~ visual perception
~ writing skills

Materials
* Ten large sheets of paper
* Felt pens

Activity
Draw one apple on the first sheet of paper, two on the second, etc. Underneath each row of apples, print the numerals 1 to 10. Child will identify how many apples are in each picture by circling the corresponding numeral, then writing the number in words below it.

34   *Matching Activities*

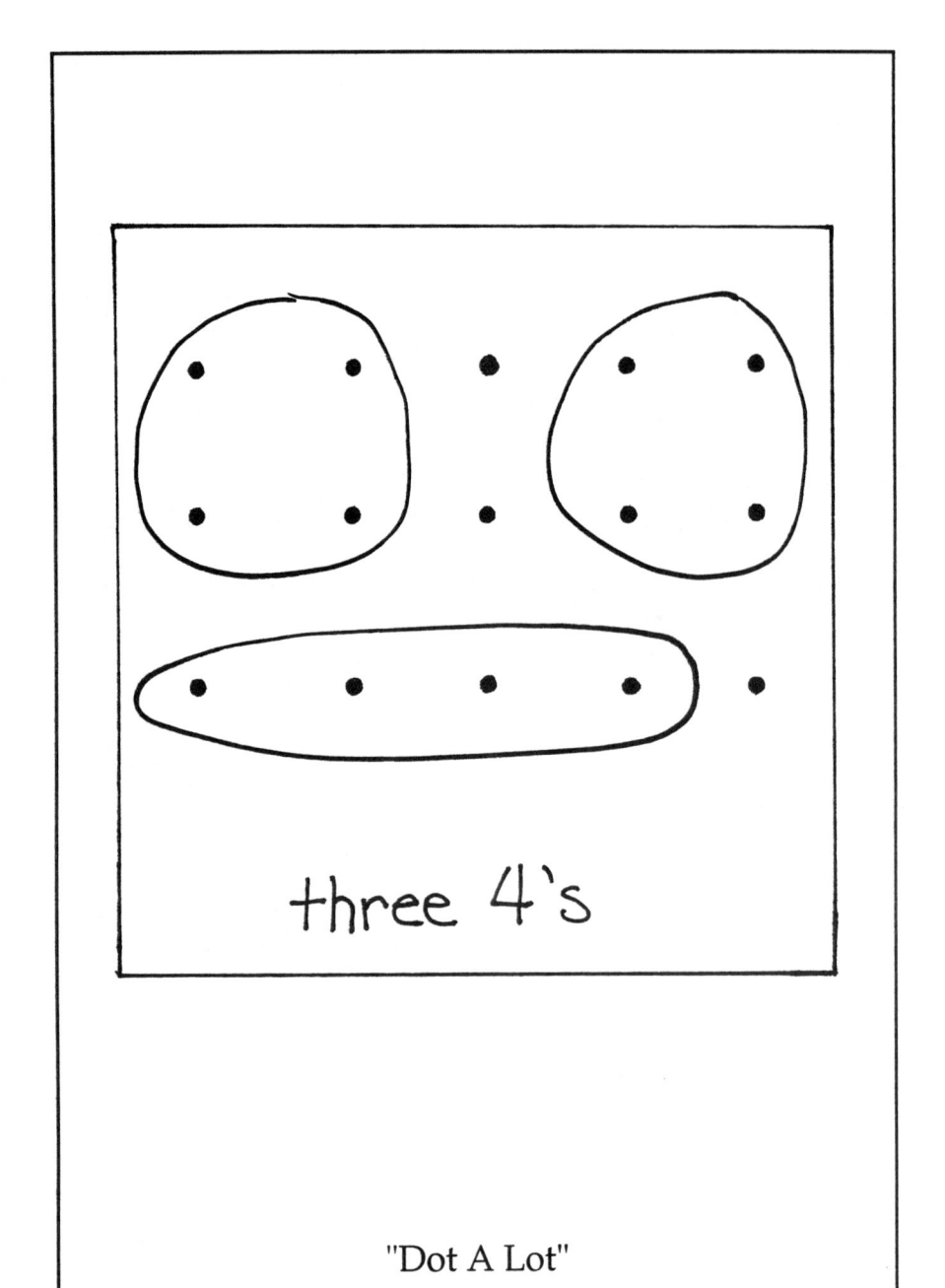

three 4's

"Dot A Lot"

"Dot A Lot"

Objectives
To promote: ~ counting skills
~ awareness of sets
~ opportunities for following directions

Materials
* Large sheet of paper
* Felt pen

Activity
Divide paper into ten equal sized squares. In each square draw fifteen large dots. Write the instruction for the number of dots to be circled underneath each group of dots, for example "two 7's", "three 4's", etc. Child will then circle the number of dots specified in each of the squares.

36 *Matching Activities*

9
nine
ninth

"Nine, Nine, Oh So Fine!"

"Nine, Nine, Oh So Fine!"

Objectives

To promote:
~ number identification
~ word recognition
~ writing skills
~ opportunities for following directions

Materials

* Sheets of paper with numerals and instructions
* Pen
* Colored pencils

Activity

Give child sheets with different numerals on them. Underneath, list a series of instructions relating to the numeral. For the number nine, for example, child could write the digit "9", write the written word "nine", write the ordinal "9th", draw nine flowers, and color nine stars.

Sequencing Numbers

The activities in this chapter emphasize the concept that numbers ascend in an equal numerical order. Different forms of numbers are introduced, enabling the child to learn connections such as "1,2,3", "1st, 2nd, 3rd", and "first, second, third". These forms are reinforced through a variety of activities that integrate counting skills, sequencing numerals, words, and ordinals.

Recommended Materials

Construction paper
Glue
Index cards
Jars or plastic containers
Marker
Newspaper
Plain paper
Deck of playing cards
Popsicle sticks
Scissors
Wire coat hanger
Wooden clothespins

44   *Sequencing Numbers*

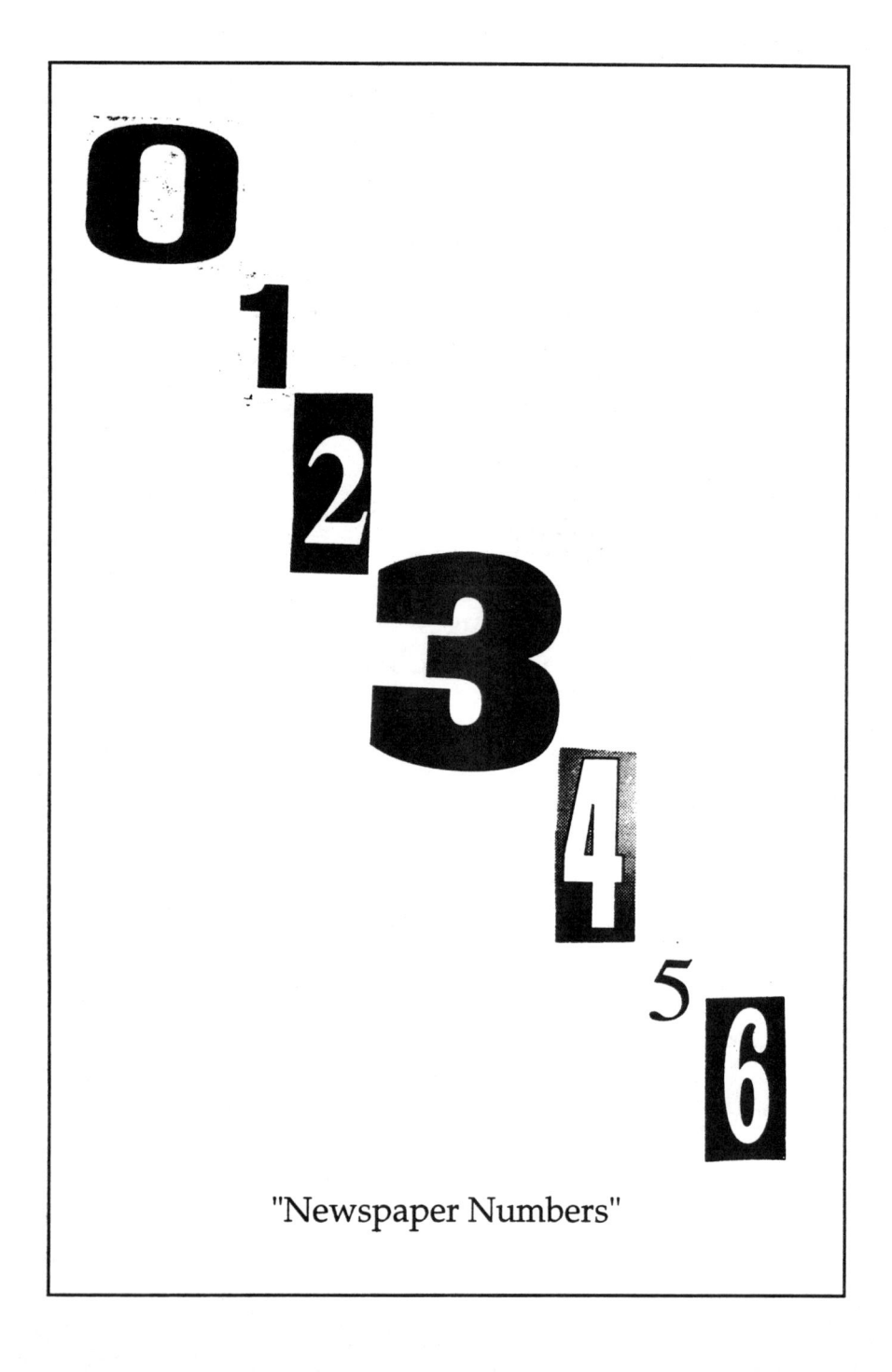

"Newspaper Numbers"

"Newspaper Numbers"

Objectives
To promote: ~ number recognition
~ sequencing skills
~ development of small motor skills

Materials
* Newspaper
* Sheet of paper
* Scissors
* Glue

Activity
Child will cut out ten numbers from the newspaper. She will then stick them on a plain sheet of paper, correctly sequenced from lowest to highest.

46   *Sequencing Numbers*

"Big, Bigger, Biggest!"

"*Big, Bigger, Biggest!*"

Objectives

To promote: ~ counting skills
~ visual discrimination
~ sequencing skills

Materials

* Ten 5 x 8 index cards
* Marker

Activity

Number index cards 1 to 10. On the reverse side of each card, write the word for the numeral in such a way that the word size increases as the number value increases. Child will sequence the cards in correct order according to the numeral on the front. Then the cards will be shuffled and child will sequence them according to the written words.

48   *Sequencing Numbers*

"Would You Like To Order?"

"Would You Like To Order?"

Objectives
To promote: ~ number identification
~ visual discrimination
~ sequencing skills
~ task completion

Materials
* Deck of playing cards

Activity
Remove face cards from deck. With aces acting as ones, child will sequence all the cards in one suit in numerical order. She will then repeat this with the other three suits until all the cards have been used.

50 *Sequencing Numbers*

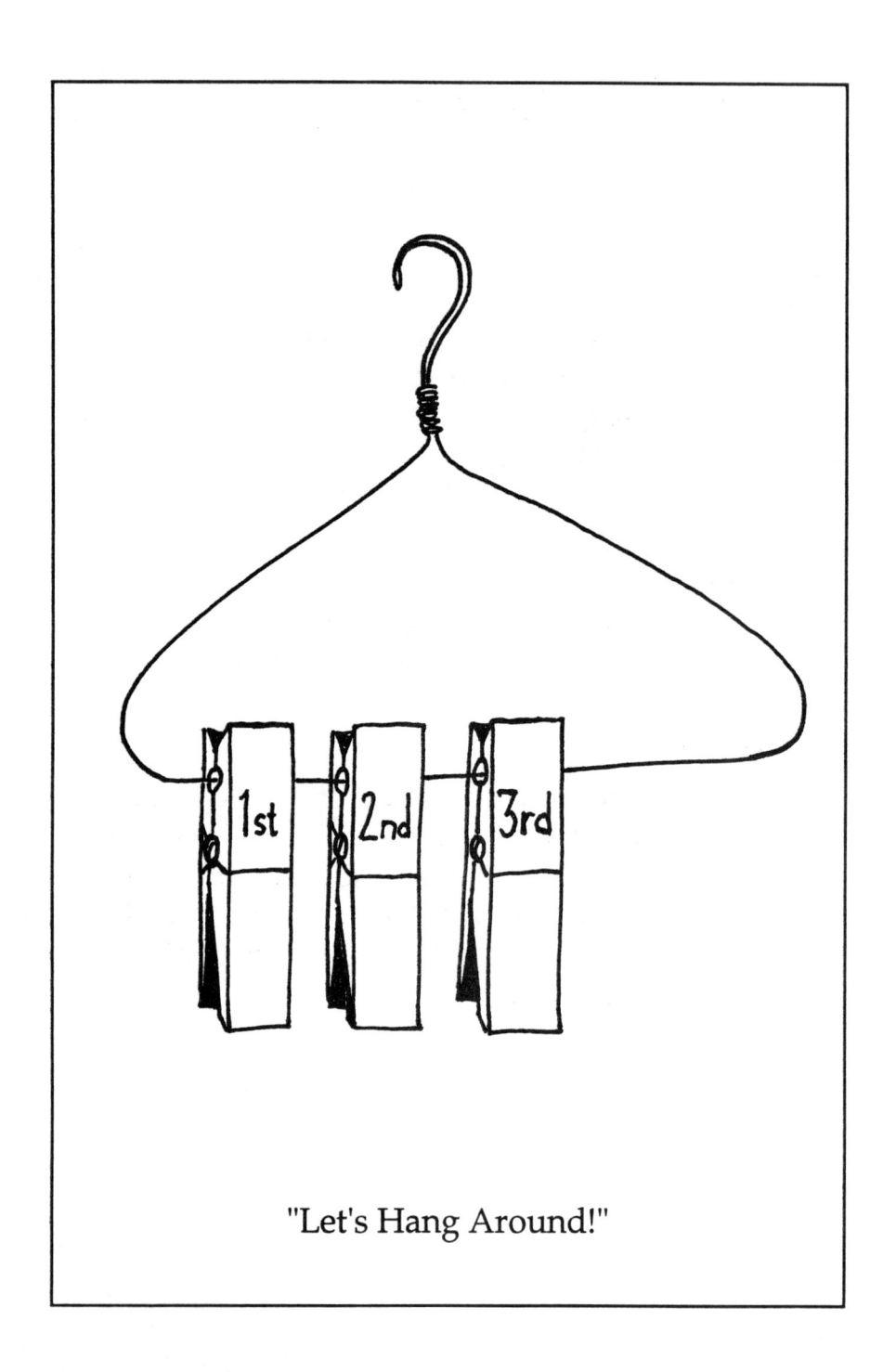

1st 2nd 3rd

"Let's Hang Around!"

"Let's Hang Around!"

Objectives
To promote: ~ number identification
~ sequencing skills
~ manipulative skills
~ eye-hand coordination

Materials
* Ten flat wooden clothespins
* Wire coat hanger
* Marker

Activity
Mark the first clothespin with ordinal "1st", the second with "2nd", etc. Child will hang clothespins off coat hanger in the correct sequence.

52   *Sequencing Numbers*

first

second

"Sweet As A Peach"

"Sweet As A Peach"

Objectives

To promote: ~ word recognition
~ matching skills
~ sequencing skills
~ manipulative skills

Materials

* Green, brown, and orange construction paper (plain paper and colored markers can be used)
* Scissors
* Marker
* Glue

Activity

Cut five trees and fifteen peaches from construction paper. Mark trees with the words "first", "second", etc. Child will stick corresponding number of peaches to each tree, then sequence the trees from first to fifth.

54   Sequencing Numbers

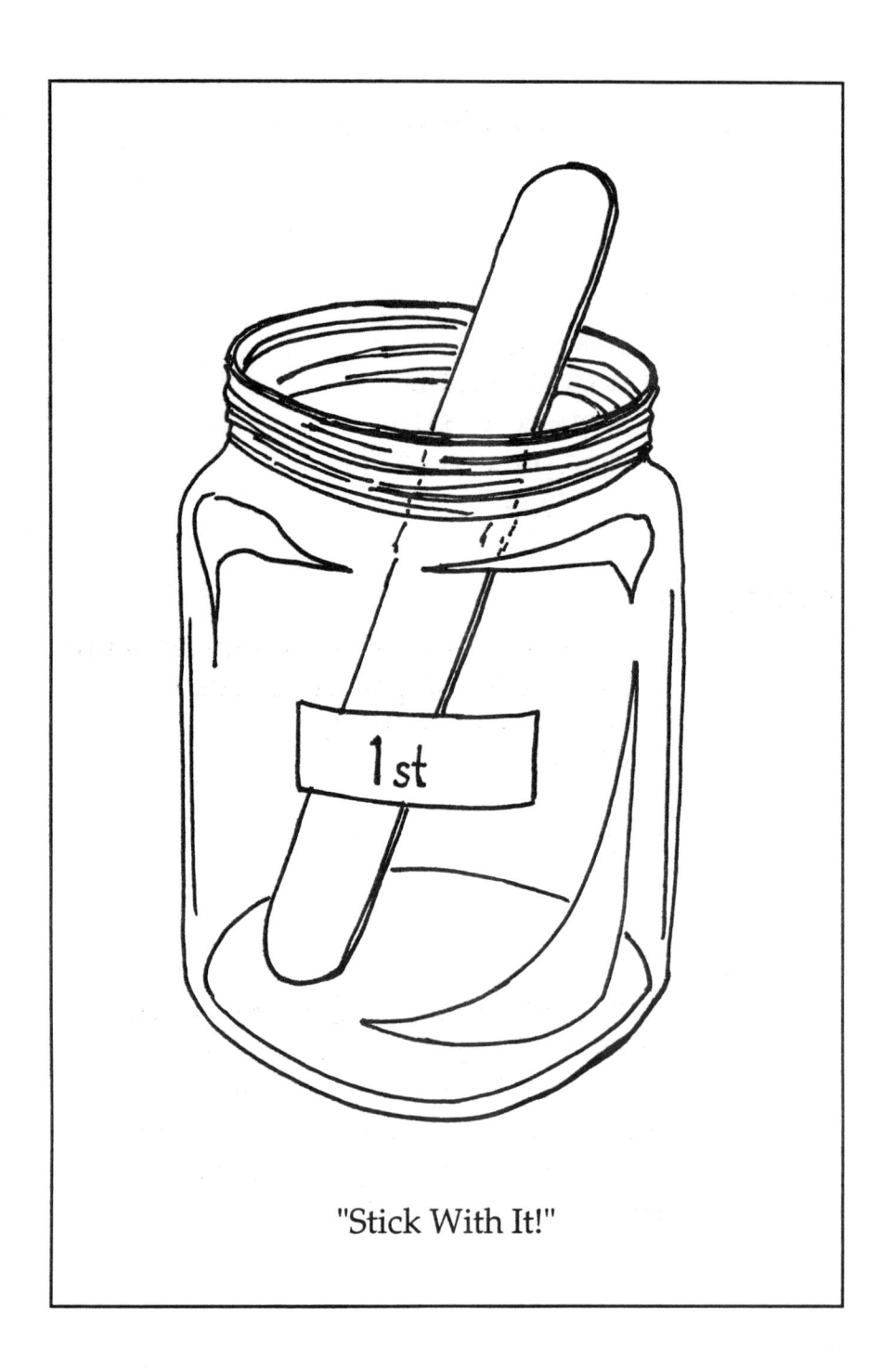

1st

"Stick With It!"

"Stick With It!"

Objectives

To promote: ~ number recognition
~ matching skills
~ sequencing skills
~ manipulative skills

Materials

* Ten plastic containers or jars
* Fifty-five popsicle sticks
* Markers (can write on masking tape and stick it on containers)

Activity

Write "1st", "2nd", etc., on containers until all ten have been labeled. Child will arrange containers in sequence, then place one popsicle stick in the first one, two in the second, etc., until all ten containers are filled.

Sorting and Classifying

Sorting and Classifying

In this chapter, the child learns to sort various objects into groups according to characteristics such as shape, color, size, and function. Comparisons are made so the child can determine which group has more than, the same as, or less than, the other group.

Some of the activities give the child the opportunity to sort objects without guidance. In such instances, it is recommended that suggestions for sorting in other ways are offered, such as color, shape, and size. This will help the child to realize that there are many different criteria that can be used to sort and classify objects.

Recommended Materials

Assortment of small objects (Ex. paper clips, beads, rubber bands, pipe cleaners, pennies, crayons, etc.)
Buttons
Construction paper
Food for snack
Plain paper
Pens
Sandwich box
Scissors
Shoes
Straws

62   *Sorting and Classifying*

"Cute As A Button"

"Cute As A Button"

Objectives

To promote: ~ sorting and classification skills
~ active exploration of materials
~ visual discrimination
~ manipulative skills

Materials

* Buttons with no holes
* Buttons with 2 holes
* Buttons with 4 holes

Activity

Give child a pile of buttons; some with no holes, some with 2 holes, and some with 4 holes. Child will sort them into three separate piles according to the number of holes in each button.

64   *Sorting and Classifying*

"Shoe Sort"

"Shoe Sort"
Activity for more than one child

Objectives
To promote: ~ sorting and classification skills
~ object identification
~ development of small motor skills
~ group cooperation

Materials
* Assortment of shoes

Activity
Children will remove shoes and sort them into separate piles according to their type. (Ex. sneakers, dress shoes, sandals). The shoes will then be put back into one pile and sorted according to how they fasten. (Ex. buckles, laces, slip-ons, Velcro).

66   *Sorting and Classifying*

"Food For Thought"

"Food For Thought"

Objectives

To promote: ~ sorting and classification skills
~ word recognition
~ counting skills
~ opportunities for following directions
~ identification of different foods

Materials

* Sandwich box
* Thirty raisins
* Sixteen peanuts
* Three carrots
* Two apples
* Paper
* Pen

Activity

Give child list of food items to be prepared as a snack (Ex. 20 raisins, 10 peanuts, 2 carrots, 1 apple). She will count out the correct number of each, and place all the food in a sandwich box. Eat and enjoy!

68 *Sorting and Classifying*

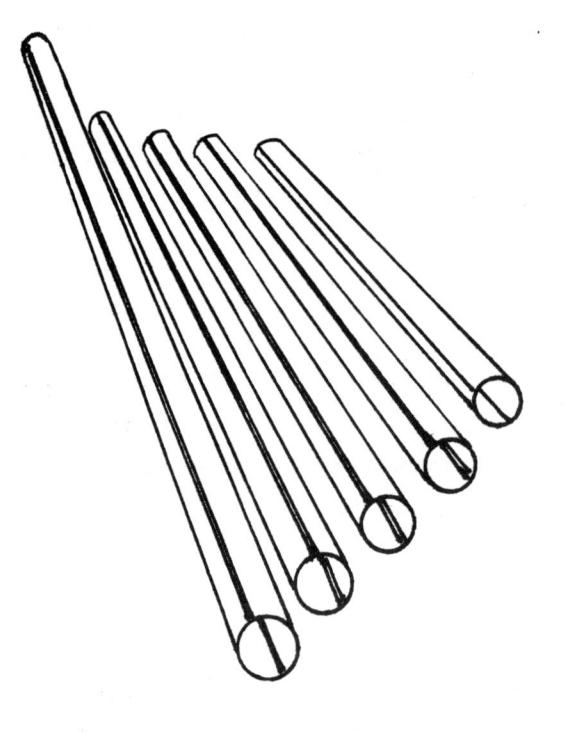

red straws

"All Sorts Of Straws"

"All Sorts Of Straws"

Objectives

To promote: ~ sorting skills
~ color identification
~ visual perception
~ manipulative skills

Materials

* Twenty-five straws in 5 different lengths and 5 different colors (permanent markers can be used to create different colors)
* Scissors

Activity

Cut five different colored straws into five different lengths and place them in a pile. Child will sort straws into five piles according to color. Straws will then be mixed back into one pile and sorted into five piles according to length.

70 *Sorting and Classifying*

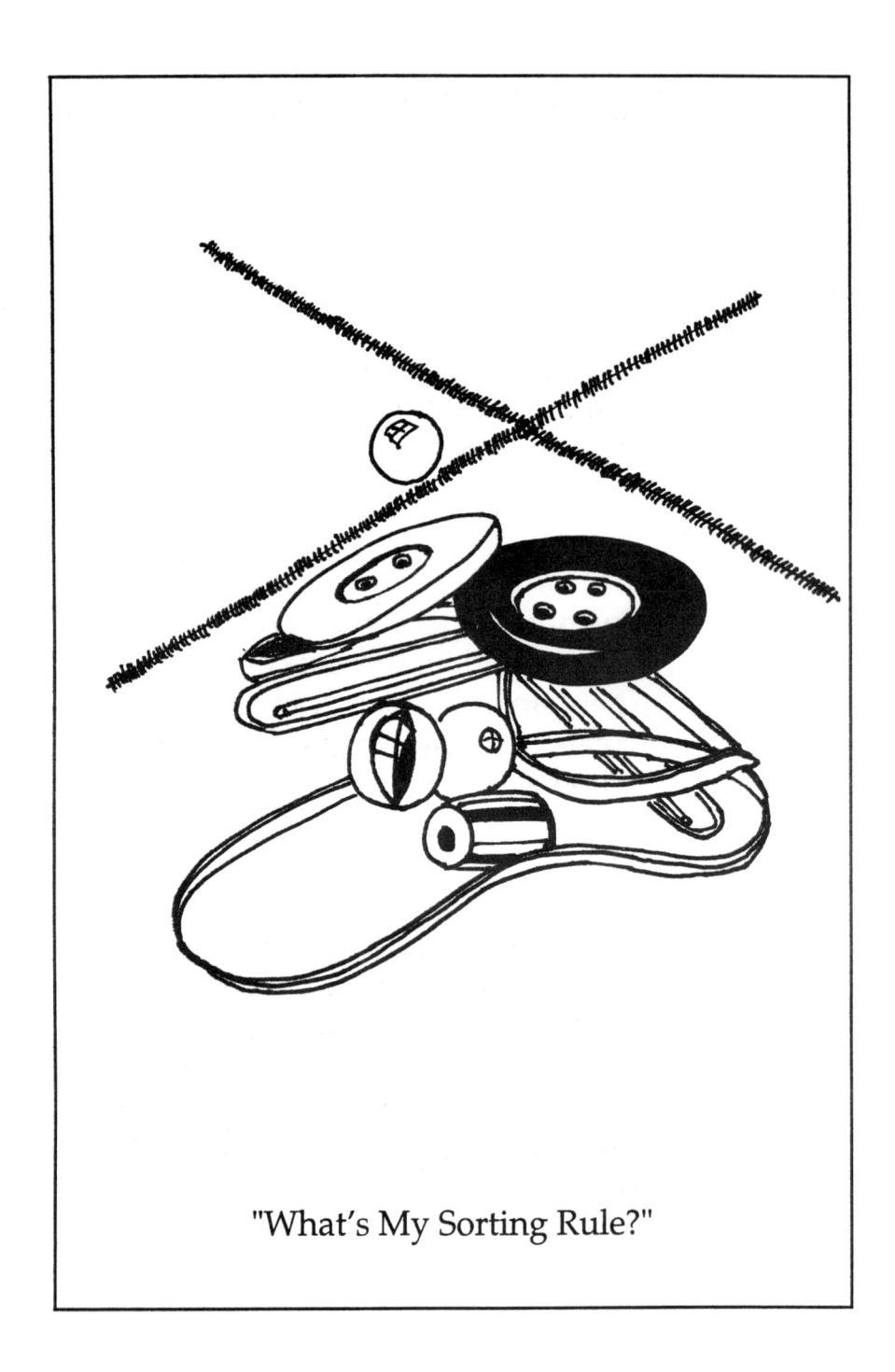

"What's My Sorting Rule?"

"What's My Sorting Rule?"
Activity for more than one child

Objectives
To promote:
~ classification skills
~ observation skills
~ object identification
~ visual discrimination

Materials
* Buttons
* Marbles
* Paper clips
* Beads
* Rubber bands
* Pipe cleaner

Activity
Display a pile of objects to children and give examples of different ways of sorting them. Then separate a number of items into a group and ask, "What's my sorting rule?" If no one guesses it, add two or three more items to the set, and ask again. Then repeat with another group of items and another sorting rule.

72   *Sorting and Classifying*

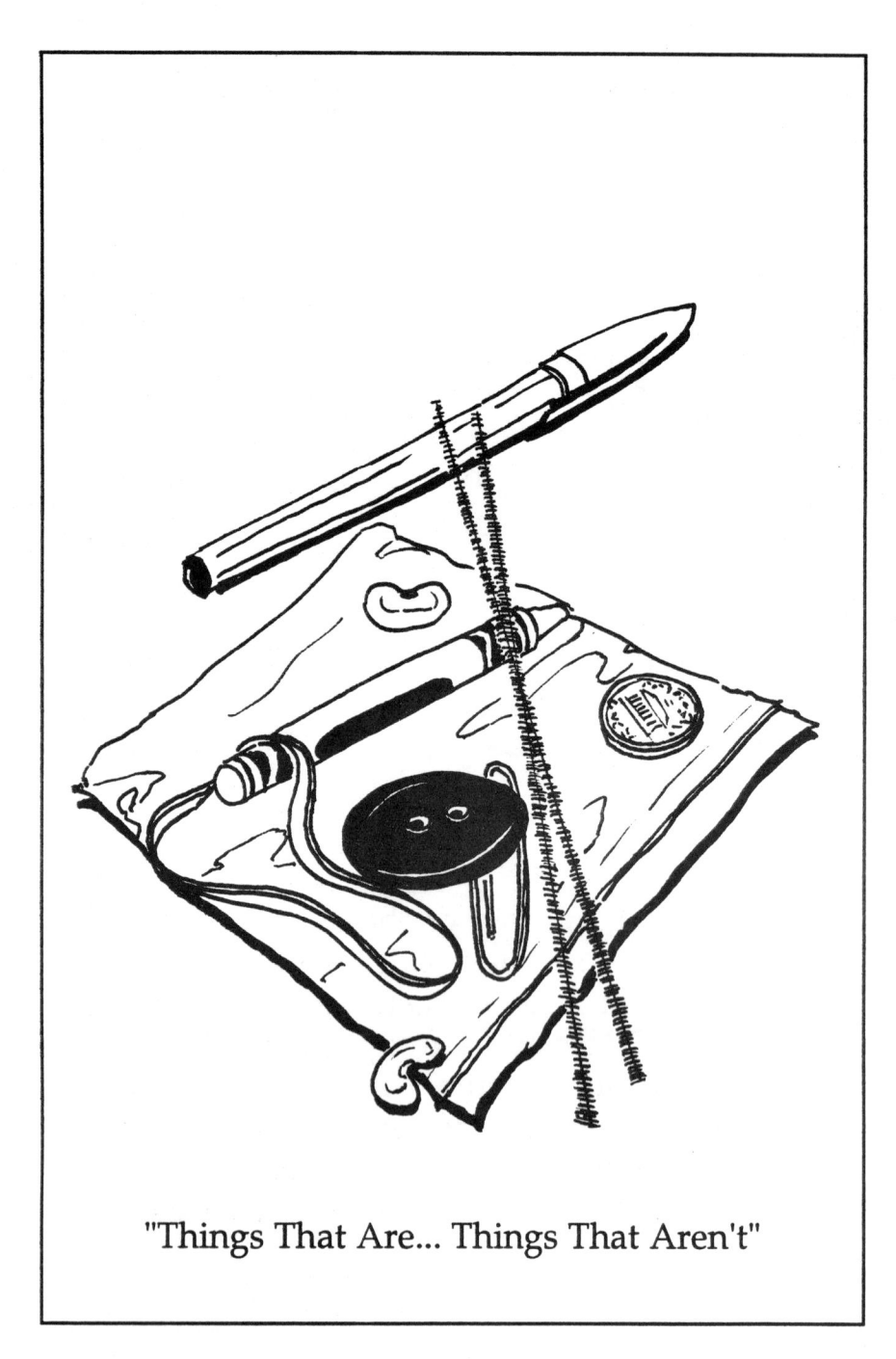

"Things That Are... Things That Aren't"

"Things That Are... Things That Aren't"

Objectives

To promote: ~ sorting and classification skills
~ active exploration of materials
~ visual discrimination

Materials

* Ziploc bag
* Paper clip
* Pipe cleaner
* Rubber band
* Crayon
* Pen
* Button
* Penny

Activity

Put various items into ziploc bag. Child will classify them according to her own criteria by using the rule "Things that are. Things that are not". For example, child may put the paper clip, pipe cleaner, and rubber band into one pile and classify them as things that fasten; the other pile will be things that do not fasten.

74   *Sorting and Classifying*

"Sizing Up Shapes"

"Sizing Up Shapes"

Objectives

To promote: ~ expansion of classification skills
~ visual discrimination
~ shape identification
~ color recognition

Materials

* Different colored construction paper
* Scissors

Activity

Cut out shapes in different sizes and colors. Child will arrange them in piles according to their shape (Ex. squares in one pile, circles in another). Then she will put them in piles according to their color. They can then be arranged in order from small to large.

Working with Shapes

Working with Shapes 79

In this chapter, basic two dimensional shapes are introduced. Activities involve using shapes in different sizes and colors so the child comes to realize that, although shapes may be presented in different forms, they are still the same due to the common geometric properties they possess.

These activities reinforce verbal and written names of shapes and lay the foundation for future geometric concepts.

Recommended Materials

Cassette of music & cassette player
Construction paper
Glue
Marker
Newpaper
Paper bag
Poster board
Scissors
Shoe boxes

82 *Working with Shapes*

"In Ship Shape"

"In Ship Shape"

Objectives
To promote: ~ shape recognition
~ sorting skills
~ manipulative skills

Materials
* Poster board
* Construction paper
* Scissors
* Glue
* Marker

Activity
Draw a circle, triangle, and square at the top of the poster board. From construction paper, cut out a variety of circles, triangles, and squares in different sizes and colors. Child will stick the shapes in the correct columns.

84   *Working with Shapes*

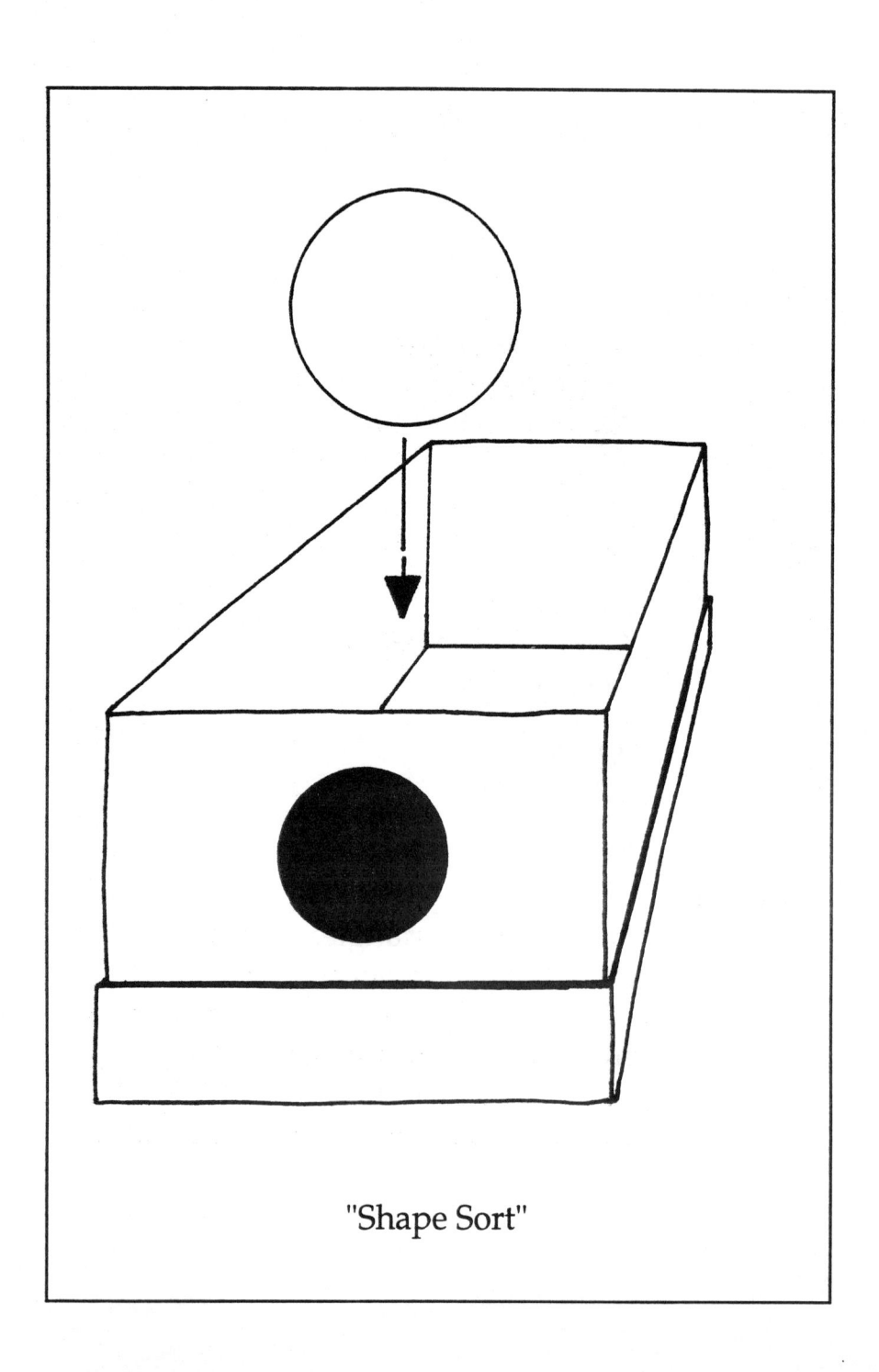

"Shape Sort"

"Shape Sort"

Objectives
To promote: ~ shape recognition
~ sorting skills
~ manipulative skills
~ visual perception

Materials
* Three shoe boxes
* Construction paper
* Paper bag
* Scissors
* Marker

Activity

Draw a different shape at the end of each shoe box. (Ex. square, triangle, circle, etc.) Cut the corresponding shapes out of construction paper and put them in a paper bag. Child will remove shapes from the bag and place them into the correct boxes.

86   *Working with Shapes*

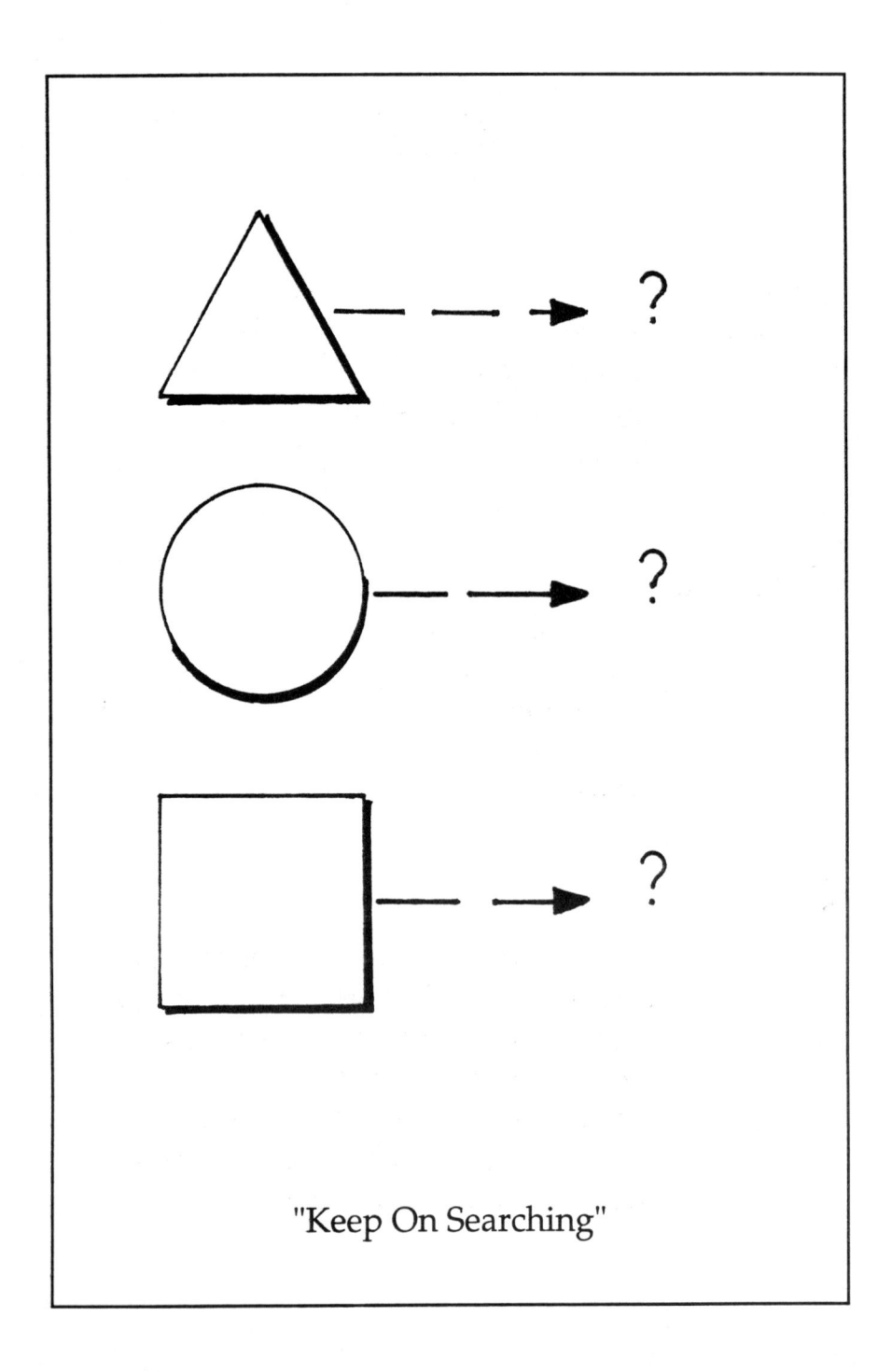

"Keep On Searching"

"Keep On Searching"

Objectives
To promote: ~ shape identification
~ matching skills
~ development of small motor skills

Materials
* Poster board
* Scissors

Activity
Cut out two circles, triangles, and squares. Hide one set of shapes around the room and give child the remaining shapes one at a time. She will use them to find the hidden shapes to create matching pairs.

88   Working with Shapes

WEATHER

Nice Day For A Great Deal

"The Shape Of Things"

"The Shape Of Things"

Objectives

To promote: ~ shape recognition
~ sorting skills
~ manipulative skills
~ visual perception

Materials

* Newspaper
* Scissors

Activity

Child will use newspaper to find pictures containing different shapes (Ex. a picture containing a square object, another containing something round). She will then cut them out and group them according to the shapes they contain.

90 *Working with Shapes*

"Step On It!"

"Step On It!"

Objectives

To promote: ~ shape identification
~ development of large motor skills
~ verbal skills

Materials

* Poster board
* Scissors
* Cassette with music
* Cassette player

Activity

From poster board, cut out several large circles, triangles, and squares and place them in a big circle on the floor. Play music. Child will walk around the circle until the music stops. Then she will name the shape on which she is standing.

92 *Working with Shapes*

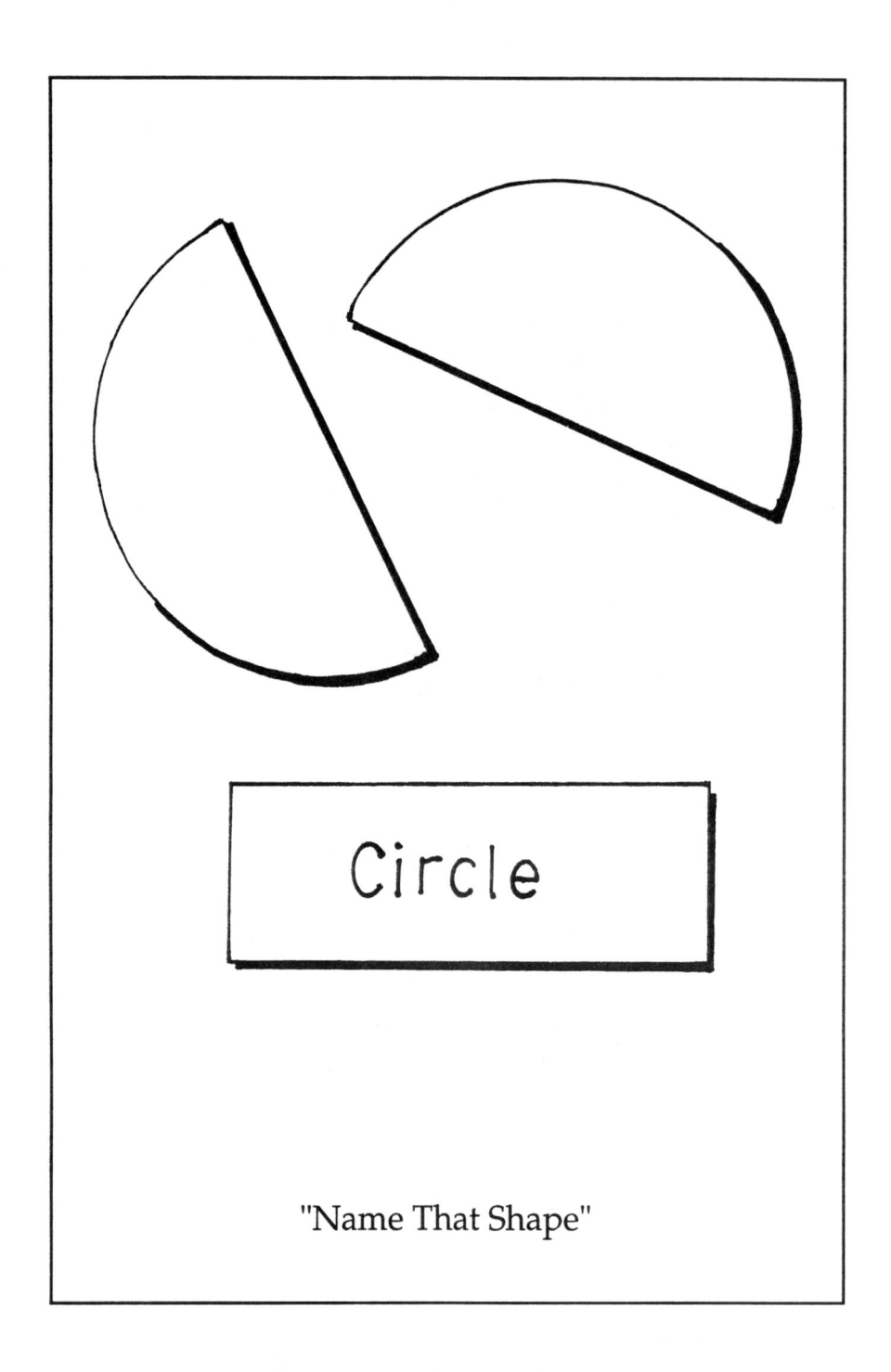

Circle

"Name That Shape"

"Name That Shape"

Objectives
To promote: ~ shape recognition
~ word recognition
~ manipulative skills

Materials
* Poster board
* Construction paper
* Scissors
* Glue
* Marker

Activity
From construction paper, cut out several squares, circles, and triangles. On poster board, draw three columns and write the names of the shapes at the top of each one. Child will stick the shapes in the corresponding columns.

Circle	Triangle	Square

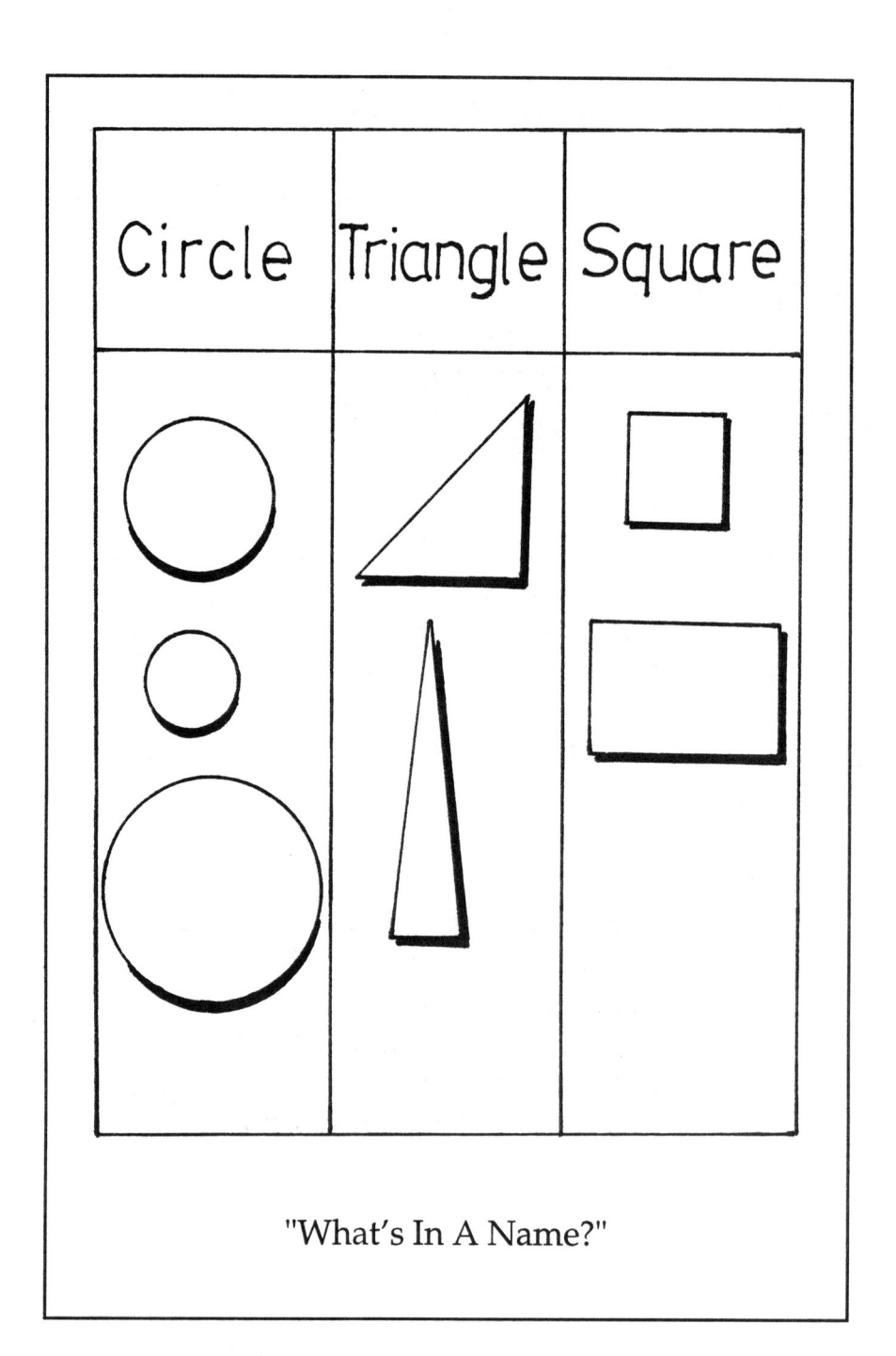

"What's In A Name?"

"What's In A Name?"

Objectives
To promote: ~ shape identification
~ matching skills
~ word recognition

Materials
* Construction paper
* Marker
* Scissors

Activity
Cut out a variety of shapes and then cut them in half. Write the names of the shapes on separate pieces of paper. Give the names and one half of each shape to the child. Child will match the shapes together and then place the correct name on each shape.

Section II

Adding Skills

In this chapter, visual images are used to introduce the child to basic addition concepts. Through the use of concrete objects, the child learns both single digit addition and regrouping skills.

All activities have been designed in such a way that the level of difficulty can be easily adapted to meet the needs of the child.

Recommended Materials

Cassette of music & cassette player
Construction paper
Dice
Egg carton
Glue
Index cards
Magazine
Marker
Masking tape
Newspaper
Plain paper
Paper cups
Pencil
Ping pong balls
Deck of playing cards
Posterboard
Scissors
Shoe holder
Large wooden beads

104 *Adding Skills*

	Which is your favorite?
Vanilla	✓ ✓ ✓
Chocolate	✓ ✓ ✓ ✓
Strawberry	✓ ✓ ✓ ✓

"Favorite Ice Cream Flavors"

"Favorite Ice Cream Flavors"
Activity for more than one child

Objectives
To promote:
~ adding skills
~ graphing skills
~ counting skills
~ reading skills
~ opportunities for individual choice

Materials
* Poster board
* Markers
* Pens

Activity
Create a chart entitled, "Favorite Ice Cream Flavors". List flavors such as vanilla, strawberry, and chocolate. Children will put a check mark in the row next to their favorite flavor. They will then add up the check marks and write down the total in each row.

106   *Adding Skills*

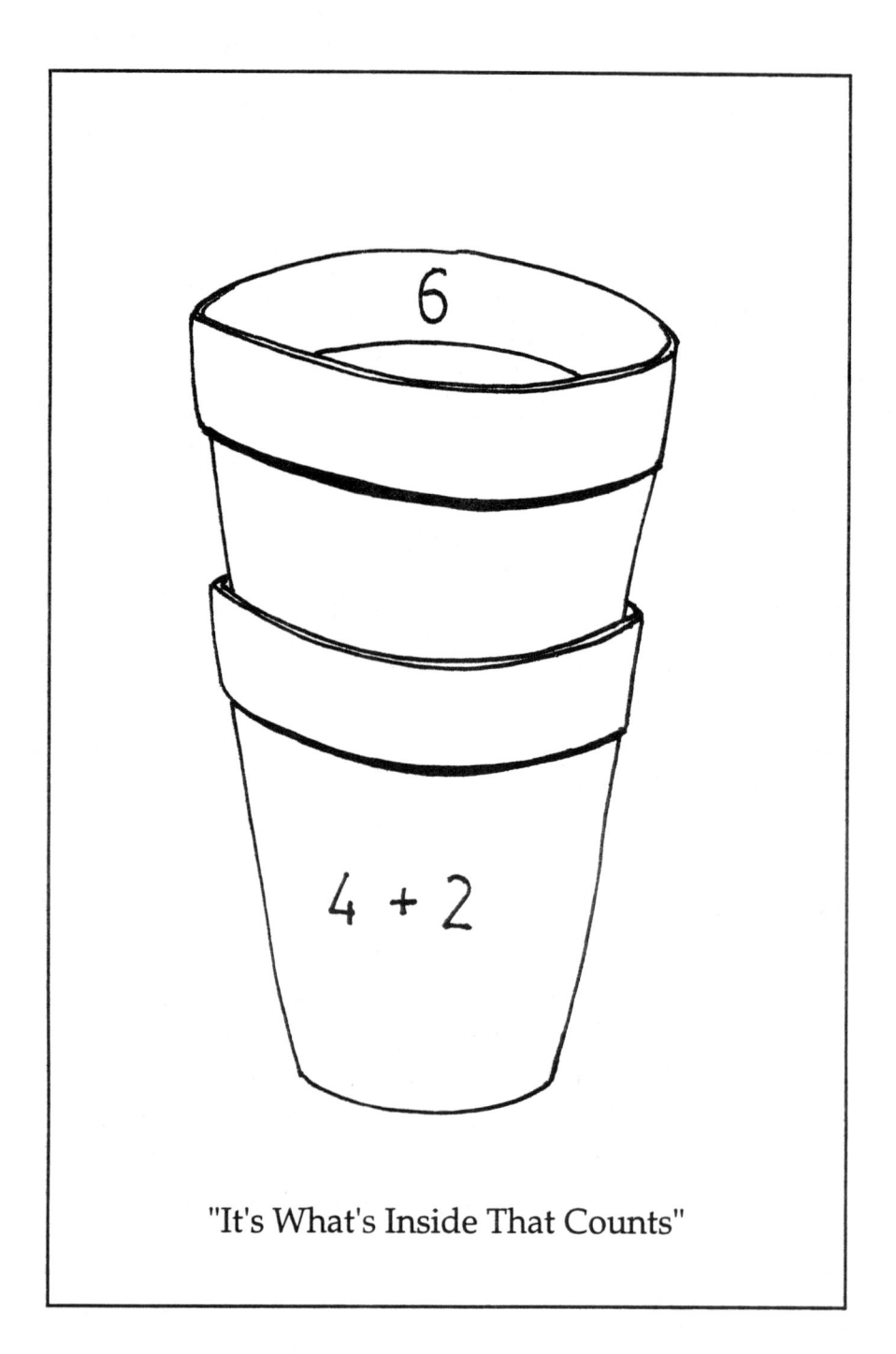

6

4 + 2

"It's What's Inside That Counts"

"It's What's Inside That Counts"

Objectives
To promote: ~ addition skills
~ number recognition
~ development of small motor skills
~ active exploration of materials

Materials
* Ten paper cups
* Marker

Activity
On the outside of half of the cups write a math problem. Write the answers to the problems on the insides of the other half. Child will match the cups together by placing the answer cup inside the question cup.

108   Adding Skills

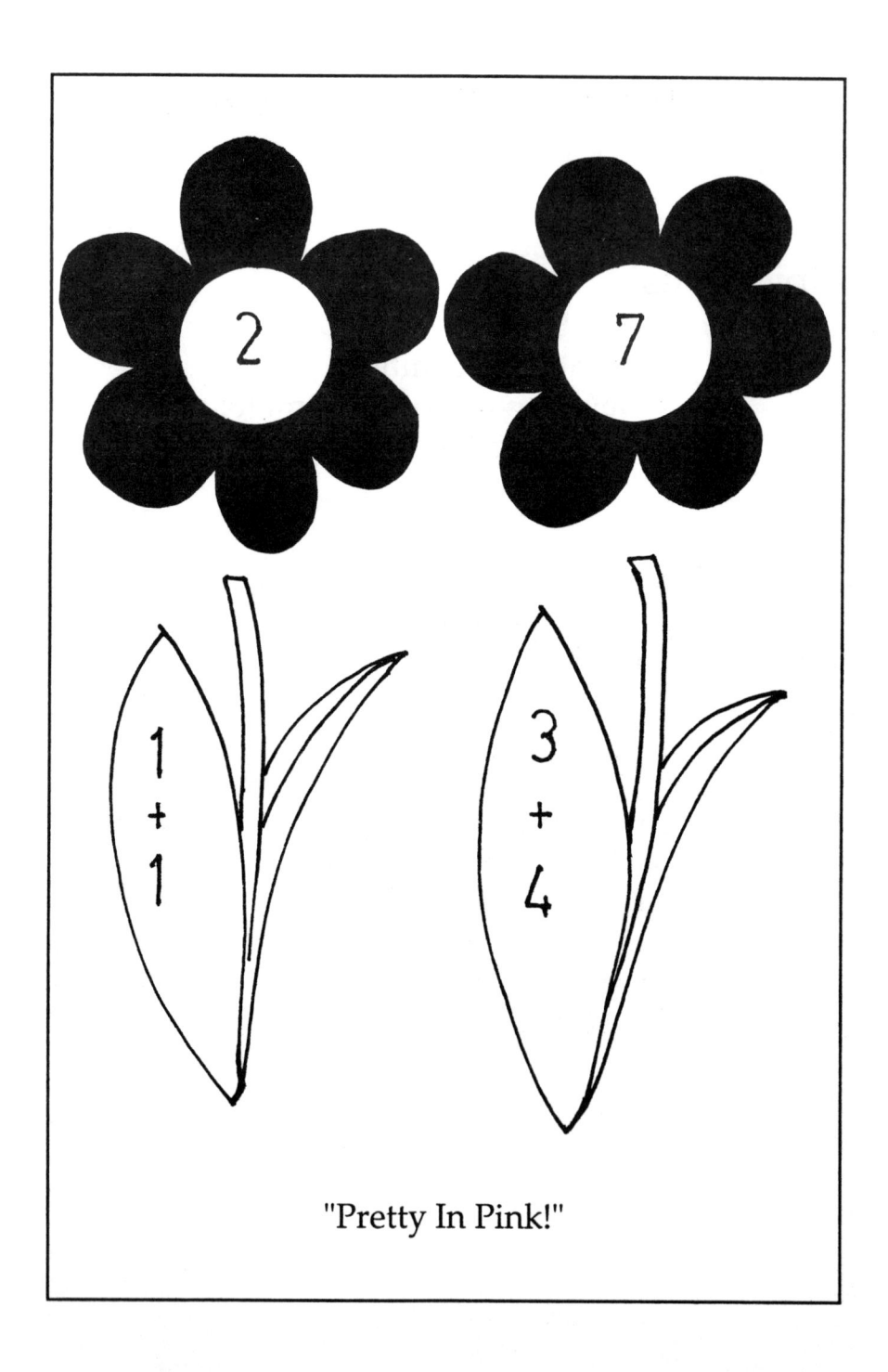

2   7

1   3
+   +
1   4

"Pretty In Pink!"

"Pretty In Pink!"

Objectives

To promote: ~ addition skills
~ number recognition
~ matching skills
~ manipulative skills

Materials

* Green and pink construction paper
* Scissors
* Marker
* Glue

Activity

Cut out flowers and flower stems from construction paper. Write addition problems on the stems and put the answers on the flowers. Child will match the stems and flowers together to correctly answer the problems.

110   *Adding Skills*

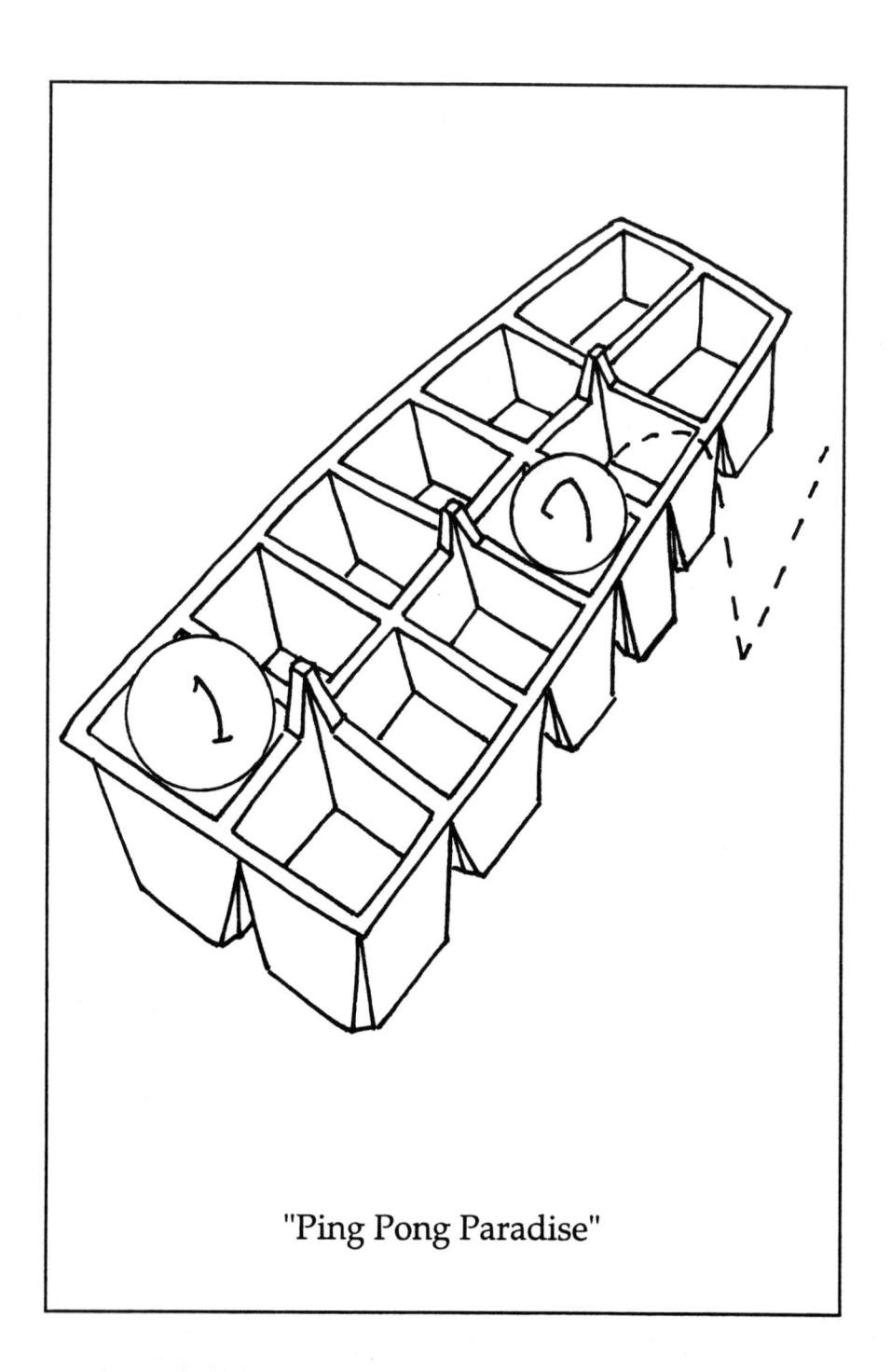

"Ping Pong Paradise"

"Ping Pong Paradise"

Objectives
To promote: ~ addition skills
~ number recognition
~ development of small motor skills

Materials
* Egg carton
* Nine ping pong balls
* Marker

Activity
Mark the first ping pong ball with the numeral "1", the second with "2", etc. Child will toss two ping pong balls into the egg carton, then add the two numbers together.

112   *Adding Skills*

"A Shoe In"

"A Shoe In"

Objectives
To promote: ~ addition skills
~ matching skills
~ visual perception
~ development of small motor skills

Materials
* Shoe holder
* Construction paper
* Scissors
* Marker

Activity
From construction paper, cut out five shoe shapes, mark them with numerals 1 to 5 and place them in a "left" pile. Do the same with five more shoes and place them in a "right" pile. Mark the pockets of the shoe holder with numerals 2 to 10. Child will select one left shoe and one right shoe, add the two numerals together, then place the pair into the pocket marked with the total number. This will be repeated until all the shoes have been placed in the shoe holder.

114   *Adding Skills*

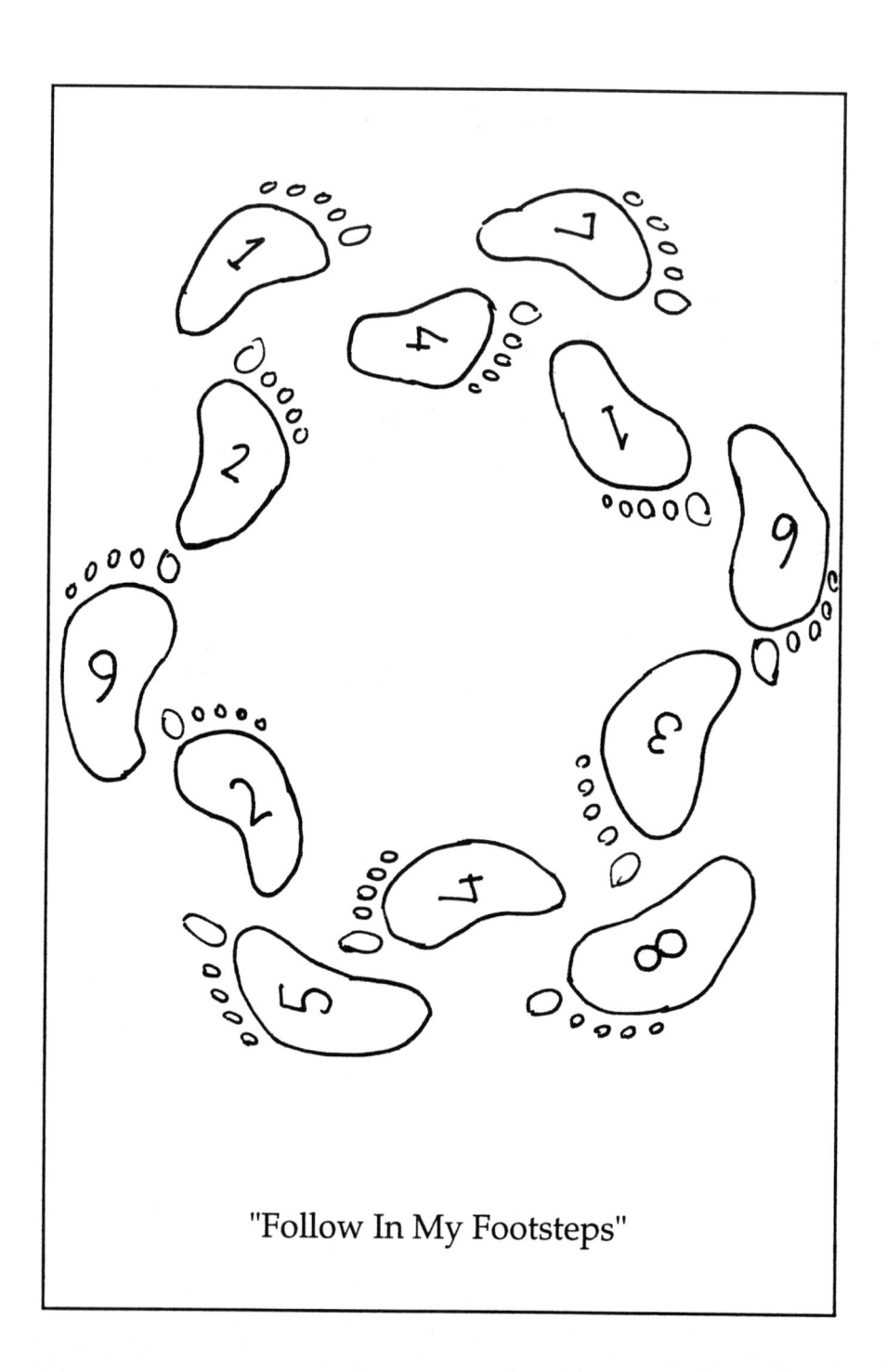

"Follow In My Footsteps"

"Follow In My Footsteps"

Objectives
To promote: ~ addition skills
~ number identification
~ development of large motor skills

Materials
* Construction paper
* Marker
* Scissors
* Masking tape
* Cassette with music
* Cassette player

Activity
From construction paper, cut out several large footstep shapes and mark a numeral on each one. Stick them down in a large circle on the floor. Play music. Child will walk around the circle, stepping on each footstep with only one foot at a time. When music stops, child will add together the numbers of the two footsteps on which she is standing.

116   *Adding Skills*

"Puppy Love"

"Puppy Love"

Objectives
To promote: ~ addition skills
~ number correspondence
~ manipulative skills

Materials
* White construction paper
* Dice
* Marker
* Scissors

Activity
Draw eleven puppies and mark them with numerals 2 to 12. Child will toss two dice, add the numbers together, then point to the puppy that is marked with the total sum.

118 Adding Skills

B	i	n	g	O
4	5	8	●	6
●	2	●	7	5
9	3	●	4	8
6	8	9	7	3
3	4	5	6	●

"Bingo Frenzy"

"Bingo Frenzy"

Objectives
To promote: ~ addition skills
~ visual and auditory perception
~ number correspondence
~ manipulative skills

Materials
* Poster board
* Markers
* Chips (coins or circles cut from card can be used)
* Scrap paper
* Pencil

Activity
On posterboard, draw squares and number them like a regular bingo board. Call two numbers to be added. Child will calculate the answer, check the board for that number, then cover it with a "chip". Game continues until all the squares are covered.

120 *Adding Skills*

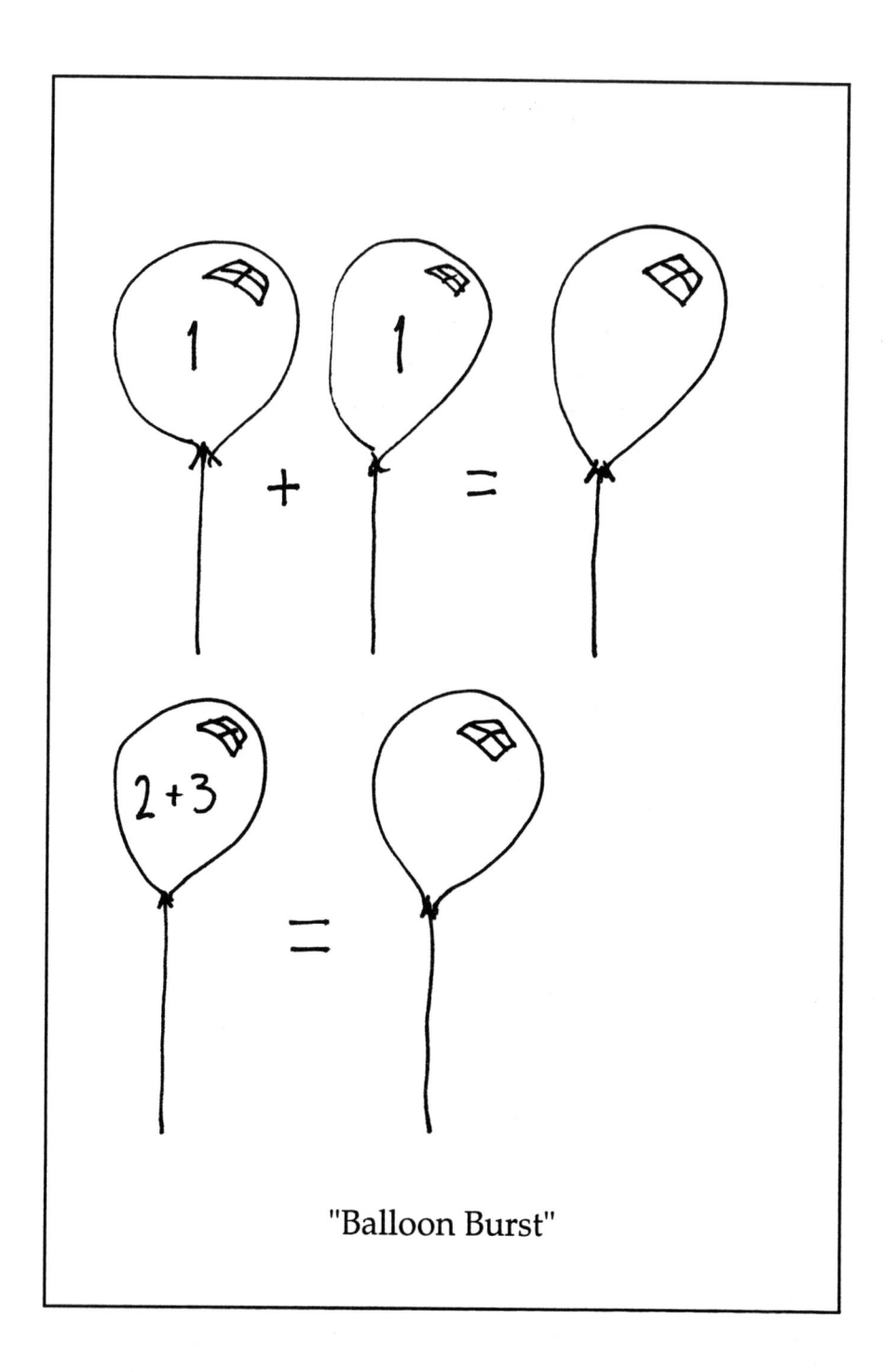

1 + 1 =

2 + 3 =

"Balloon Burst"

"Balloon Burst"

Objectives
To promote: ~ addition skills
~ number recognition
~ practise in writing numbers

Materials
* Poster board
* Markers
* Pencil

Activity
Draw balloons with addition problems on them and draw an empty balloon next to each one. Child will write the answer to each problem on the empty balloon.

122 *Adding Skills*

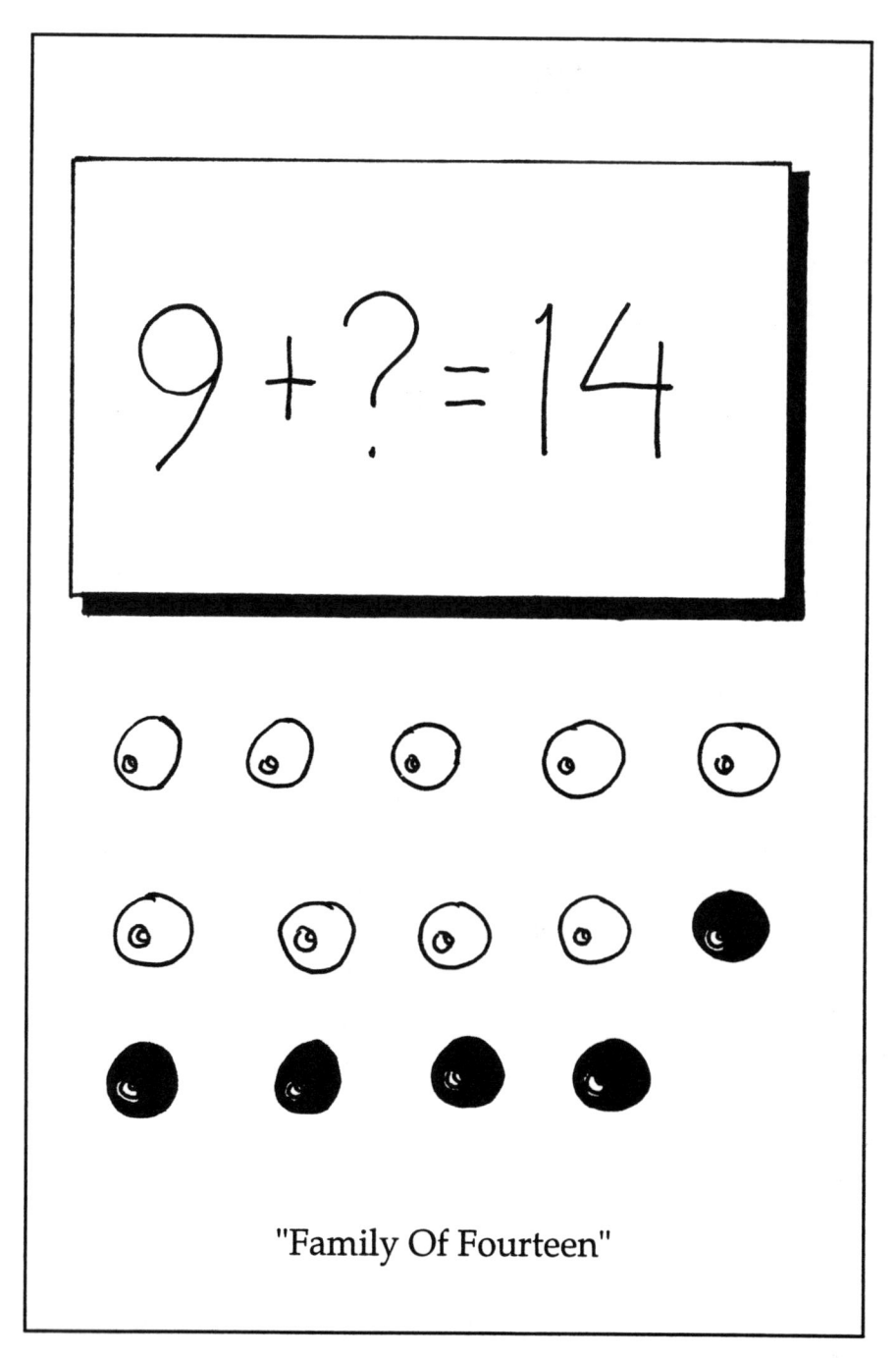

$$9 + ? = 14$$

"Family Of Fourteen"

"Family Of Fourteen"

Objectives
To promote:
~ addition skills
~ problem-solving strategies
~ logical reasoning
~ manipulative skills

Materials
* 3 x 5 index cards
* Markers
* Large wooden beads

Activity
Using numbers under fourteen, write out addition equations on index cards. Using beads as counting aids, child will find the number that makes the equation equal fourteen.

124   *Adding Skills*

"What's In The Cards?"

"What's In The Cards?"
Activity for more than one child

Objectives
To promote: ~ addition skills
~ visual perception
~ cooperation

Materials
* Deck of playing cards

Activity
Remove face cards and aces from deck and turn all the cards face down. Children will take turns flipping over two cards. If the numerals on the cards match, the cards will be put to one side. If they do not match, the two numbers will be added together and the cards turned face down again. Game continues until all the cards have been paired up.

126   *Adding Skills*

"Card Collection"

"Card Collection"
Activity for more than one child

Objectives
To promote: ~ addition skills
~ opportunities for taking turns
~ understanding of place value

Materials
* Deck of playing cards
* Scrap paper
* Pencil

Activity
Remove face cards and aces from deck and divide cards equally among children. Each child will turn over two cards and add them together. The child with the highest total wins all the cards in that round. In the event of a tie, a third card is turned over and added to the other two. The object of the game is to collect all the cards in the deck.

128   *Adding Skills*

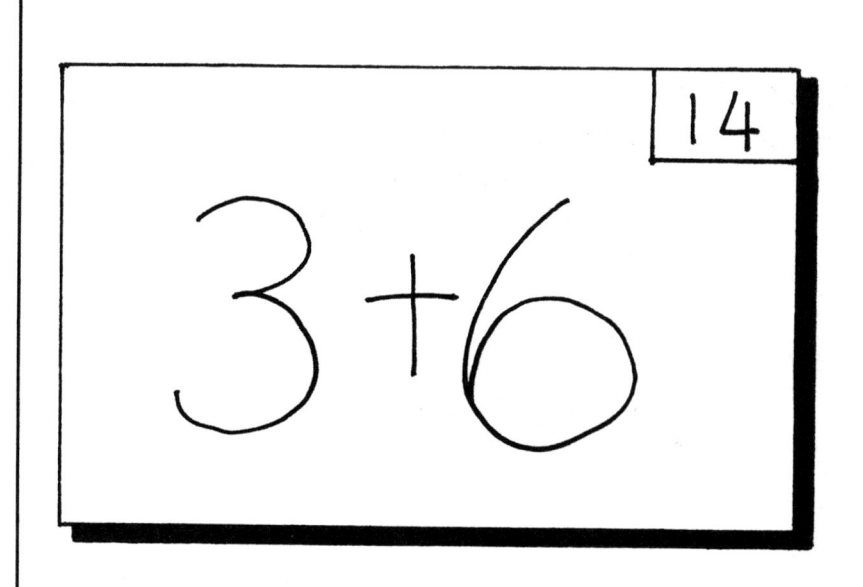

	14
$3+6$	

"Who's Got The Answer?"

"Who's Got The Answer?"
Activity for more than one child

Objectives
To promote: ~ addition skills
~ group participation
~ development of verbal skills

Materials
* 3 x 5 index cards

Activity
Write addition problems on index cards. Each card will have the answer to a different problem printed in the corner. Give each child a card. The first child will stand up and read out her question. The child who has the answer to the question written in the corner of her card stands up. First she will read out the correct answer, then she will read out her question. This will be answered by another child. Game ends when everyone has had a turn.

130   *Adding Skills*

7:00 P.M.

②EXTRA: The Entertainment Magazine
James Woods. 8057

❸ Movie
★★ *Napoleon And Samantha* (1972, adventure) Michael Douglas, Johnny Whitaker, Jodie Foster. An Oregon farm boy and his girlfriend run off with a circus lion to find a reclusive friend. (Part 2 of 2) (1 hr.) 8811

④ Paid Programming 4521

❺ Musicworks 2569

❻ ㊸ Hypertension: Down With High Blood Pressure Learning to control your blood pressure. 3811 309683

⑦ ⑬ News 📺 7637 3416960

⑧ Wheel Of Fortune 📺 7724366

❾ ❿ Babylon 5 A pilgrim (David Warner) seeks the Grail on Babylon 5; a criminal monstrously eliminates witnesses. 📺 87298 78540

❿ College Show 3429434

⓫ Missing Children Non-custodial parents abduct children in Ontario; parents establish a centre to search for son. 1095

⑪ Star Trek: The Next Generation Picard travels through time trying to prevent himself from destroying humanity. (Part 2 of 2) (R) 📺 72366

⓬ To Be Announced 9637

$$\begin{array}{r} 2 \\ 3 \\ +4 \\ \hline 9 \end{array}$$

"Prime Time"

"Prime Time"

Objectives
To promote: ~ addition skills
~ reading skills
~ manipulative skills
~ visual perception

Materials
* Newspaper
* Scissors
* Scrap paper

Activity
Give child newspaper. She will use the television pages to find three channels that have a program beginning at 7pm. She will then add the channel numbers together to find the total number.

132   *Adding Skills*

"Where's That Number?"

"Where's That Number?"

Objectives
To promote: ~ addition skills
~ number identification
~ visual perception
~ perseverance

Materials
* Colorful picture (can be cut out of a magazine)
* Markers
* Scrap paper
* Pencil

Activity
Write five numbers on a colorful picture. Child will find the hidden numbers and add them all together.

Adding Skills

$400 + 500 + 100 = 1000$

$1 + 1 = 2$

$5 + 6 = \underline{11}$

$9 + 2 + 1 = \underline{12}$

$15 + 12 = \underline{27}$

$2 + 2 + 2 = \underline{6}$

$33 + 5 + 2 + 1 = \underline{41}$

$3 + 2 + 1 + 4 = \underline{10}$

$4 + 4 + 4 + 4 = \underline{16}$

$7 + 11 = \underline{18}$

$2 + 2 = \underline{4}$

$100 + 56 + 2 = \underline{158}$

$55 + 3 + 8 = \underline{66}$

$22 + 45 + 165 = \underline{?}$

$$\begin{array}{r}15\\15\\+15\\\hline 45\end{array}$$

$6 + 7 + 5 + 2 = \underline{20}$

$$\begin{array}{r}2\\1\\+18\\\hline 21\end{array}$$

$10 + 3 + 2 = \underline{15}$

"Math Mural"

"Math Mural"
Activity for more than one child

Objectives
To promote: ~ addition skills
~ writing skills
~ cooperation
~ task commitment

Materials
* Largest piece of paper that will fit on wall
* Markers

Activity
Children work in pairs. One child will write an addition problem for the other. When the question is answered by the partner, the second child will write a problem for the first child. This continues until the paper is filled.

Subtracting Skills

The activities in this chapter build upon the addition skills acquired in the previous chapter. These activities reinforce numeration and place value through concrete representation.

The use of familiar objects is combined with abstract written forms to provide the child with a firm understanding of subtraction concepts.

Recommended Materials

Buttons
Assortment of coins
Construction paper
Dice
Egg carton
Index cards
Marker
Newspaper
Plain paper
Paper bags
Pen
Pencils
Deck of playing cards
Scissors

142   *Subtracting Skills*

"Who's Left?"

"Who's Left?"

Objectives
To promote: ~ subtraction skills
~ counting skills
~ visual perception

Materials
* Newspaper
* Scissors

Activity
Cut out picture from newspaper showing a group of people. Ask child how many people she can see. Tell her that you want to see a lower number. She will then cover the picture (a small piece of card can be used) so that only the required number is visible.

144   *Subtracting Skills*

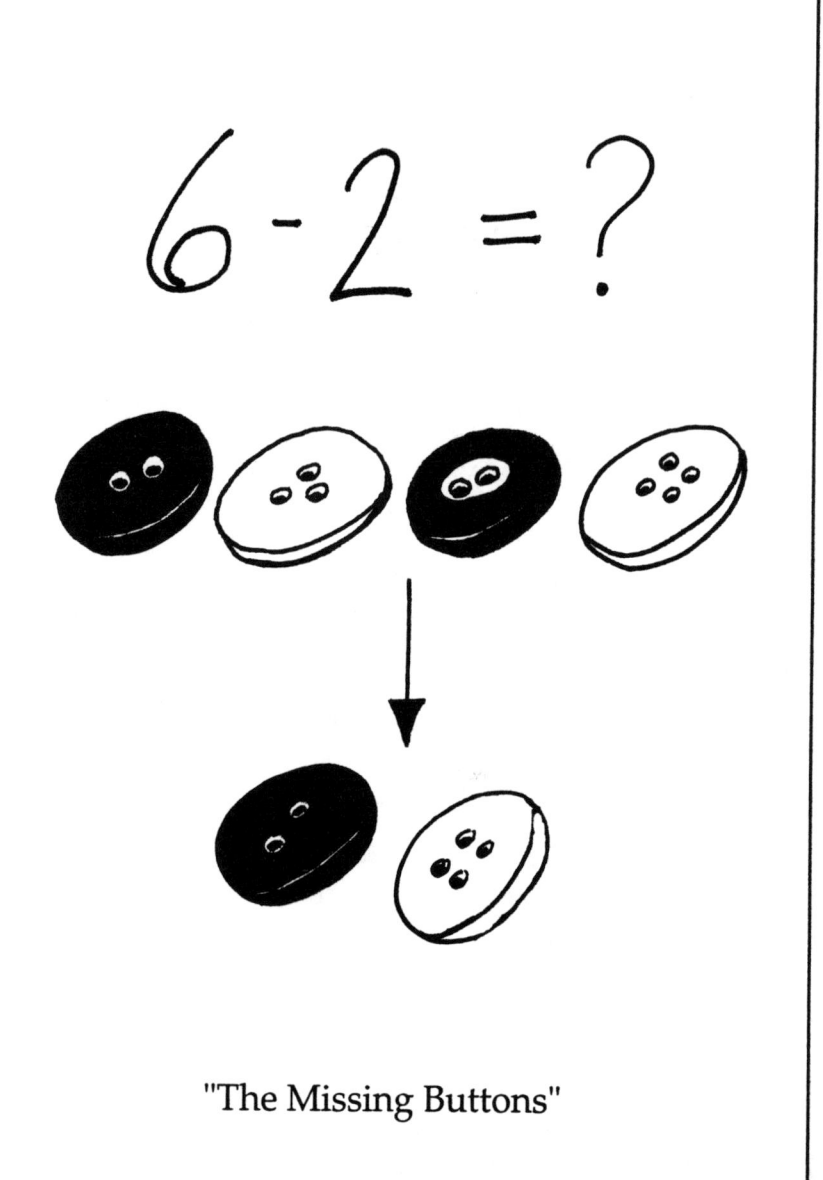

$$6 - 2 = ?$$

"The Missing Buttons"

"The Missing Buttons"

Objective
To promote: ~ subtraction skills
~ visual perception
~ active exploration of materials
~ development of small motor skills

Materials
* Buttons
* Paper
* Pen

Activity
Give child assortment of buttons. Write out a subtraction problem. Using buttons, child will demonstrate how to solve the problem. (Ex. "6 - 2": Child will line up 6 buttons, then remove 2 of them).

146 *Subtracting Skills*

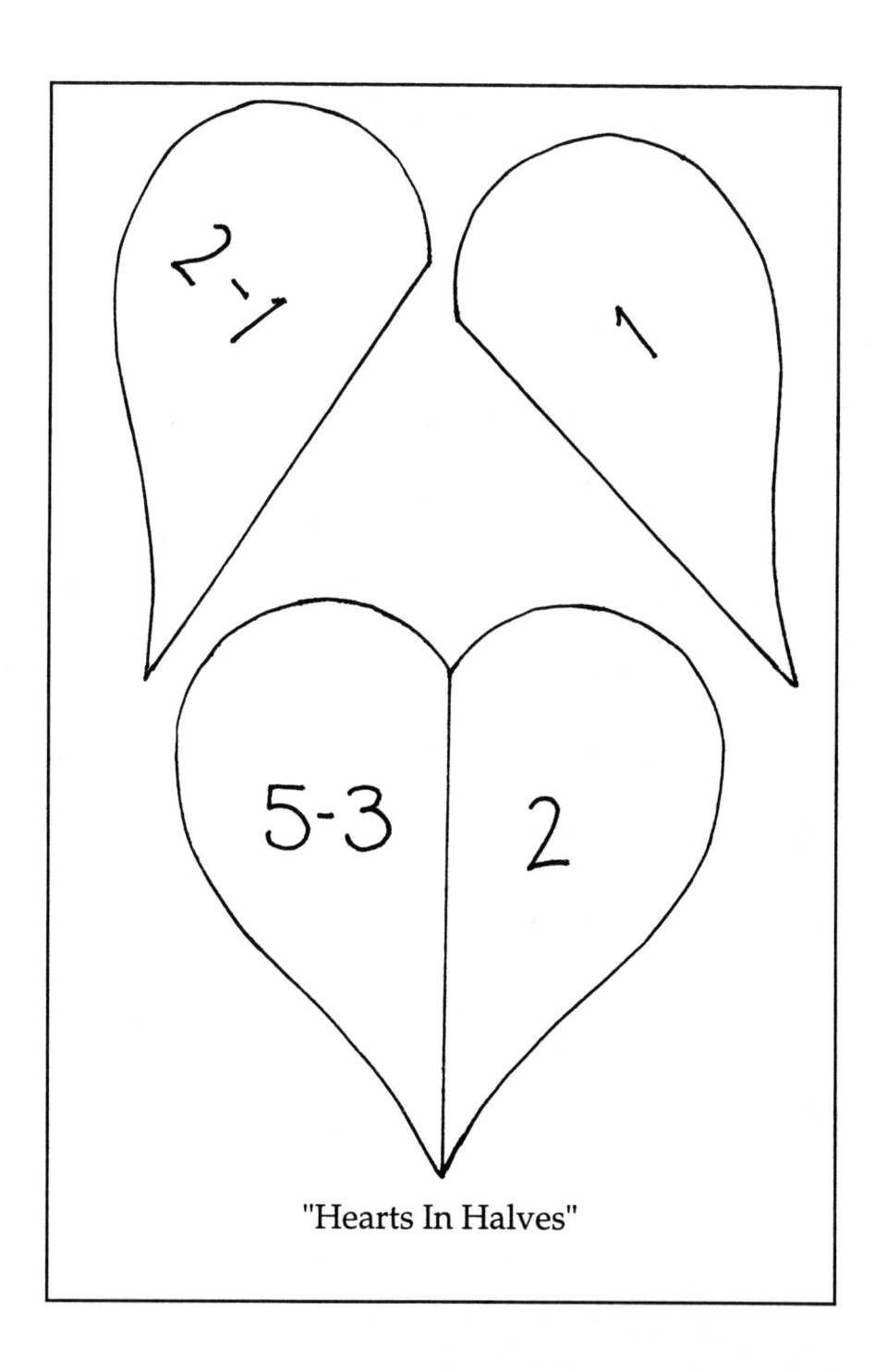

"Hearts In Halves"

"Hearts In Halves"

Objectives
To promote: ~ subtraction skills
~ manipulative skills
~ development of small motor skills

Materials
* Red construction paper
* Marker
* Scissors

Activity

Cut out ten hearts from construction paper. Cut hearts in half and write subtraction problems on one half, and answers on the other half. Separate the pieces. Child will match the halves together to correctly answer the sums.

148   *Subtracting Skills*

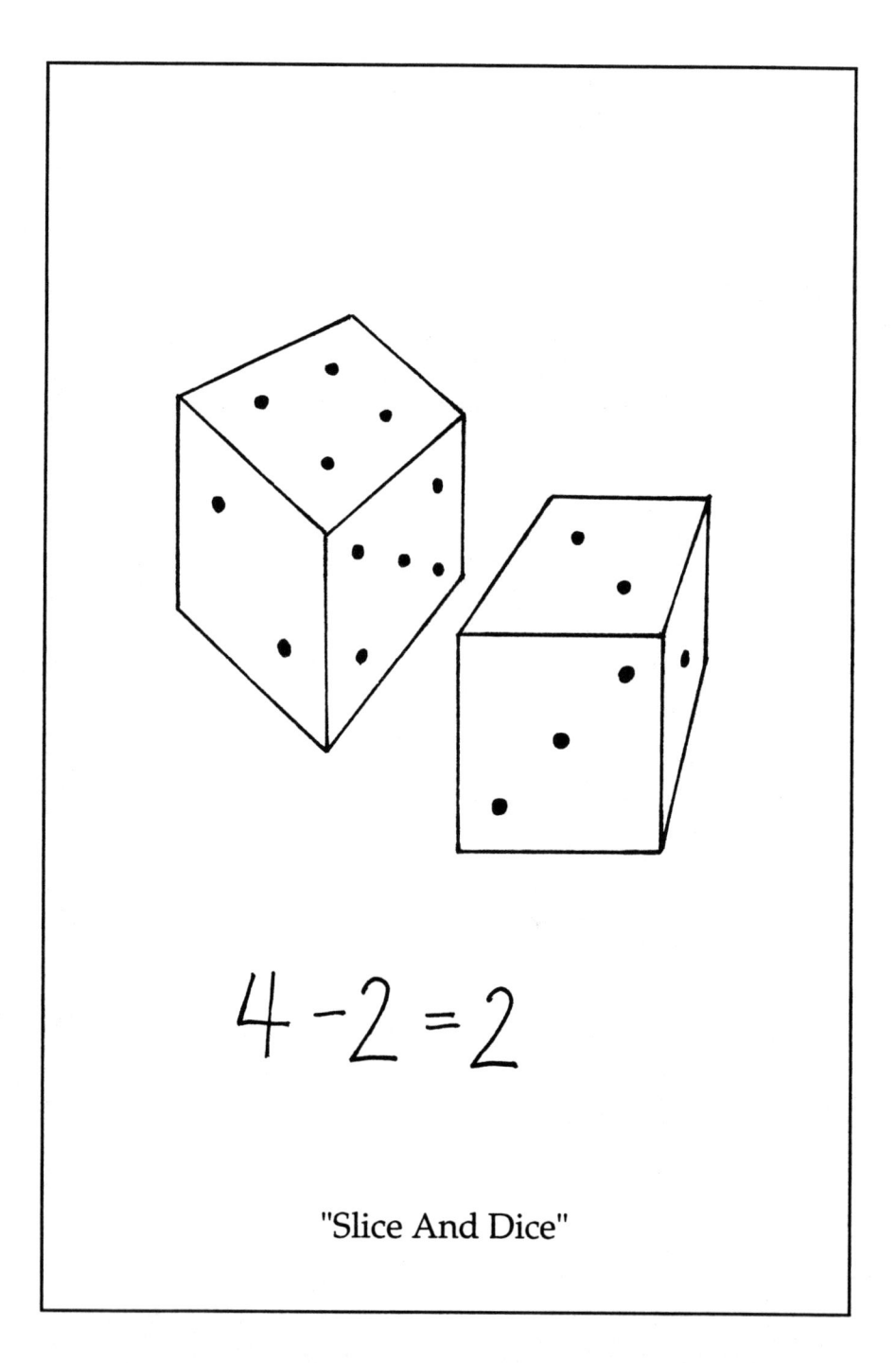

$$4 - 2 = 2$$

"Slice And Dice"

"Slice And Dice"

Objectives
To promote: ~ subtraction skills
~ number recognition
~ development of small motor skills

Materials
* Two large dice

Activity
Child will throw two dice and subtract the lower number from the higher number. In the event of the same number appearing, child will throw one of the dice again.

150   *Subtracting Skills*

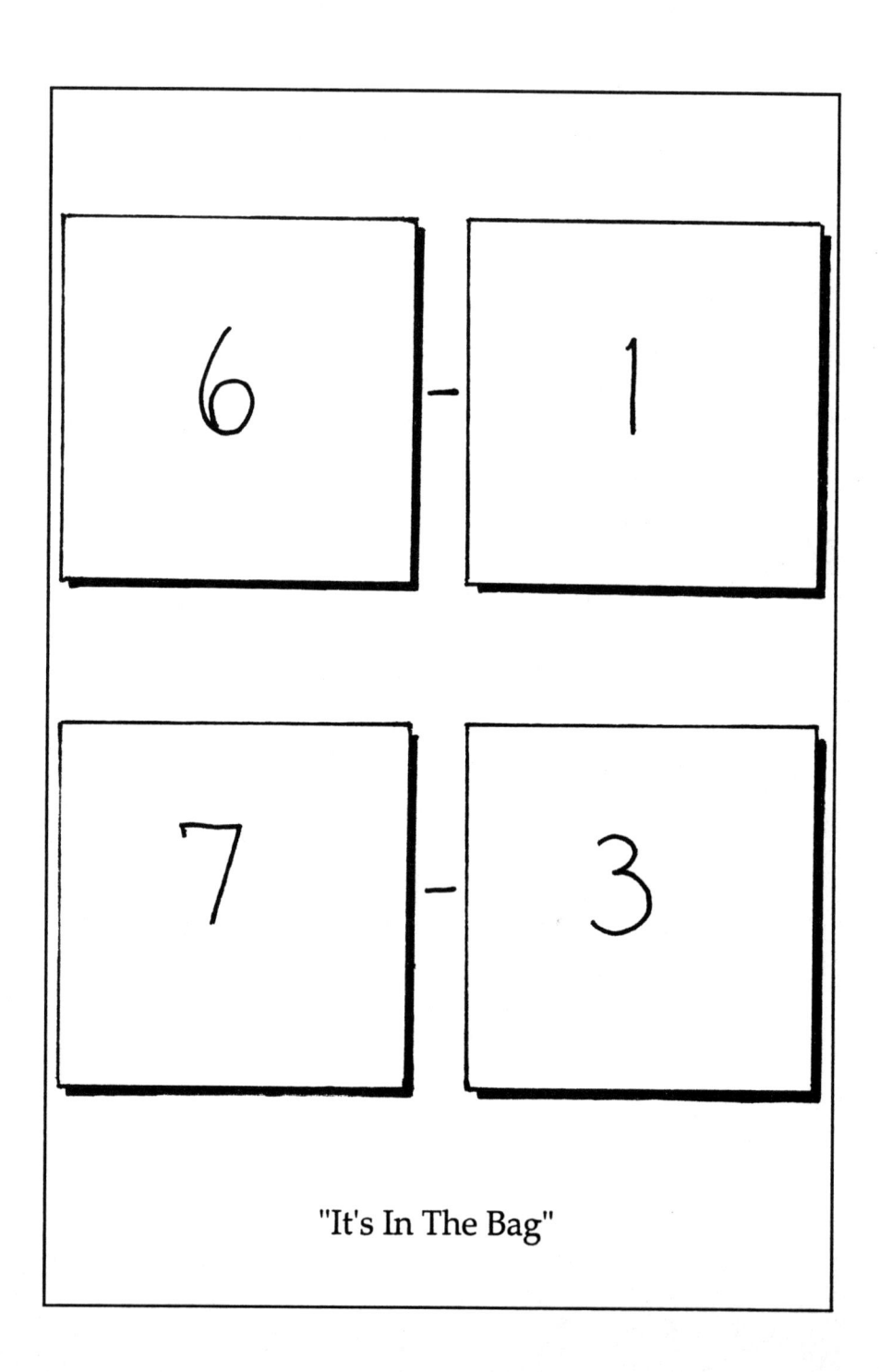

6 − 1

7 − 3

"It's In The Bag"

"It's In The Bag"

Objectives
To promote:
~ subtraction skills
~ development of small motor skills
~ task completion

Materials
* Construction paper
* Two paper bags
* Marker
* Scissors

Activity
Cut out ten paper squares. Mark numerals 1 to 5 on half of them, and place them in a bag. Then mark numerals 6 to 10 on the other half, and put them in another bag. Child will pick one number from each bag and subtract the lower number from the higher number. This will be repeated until all the squares are used up.

152   *Subtracting Skills*

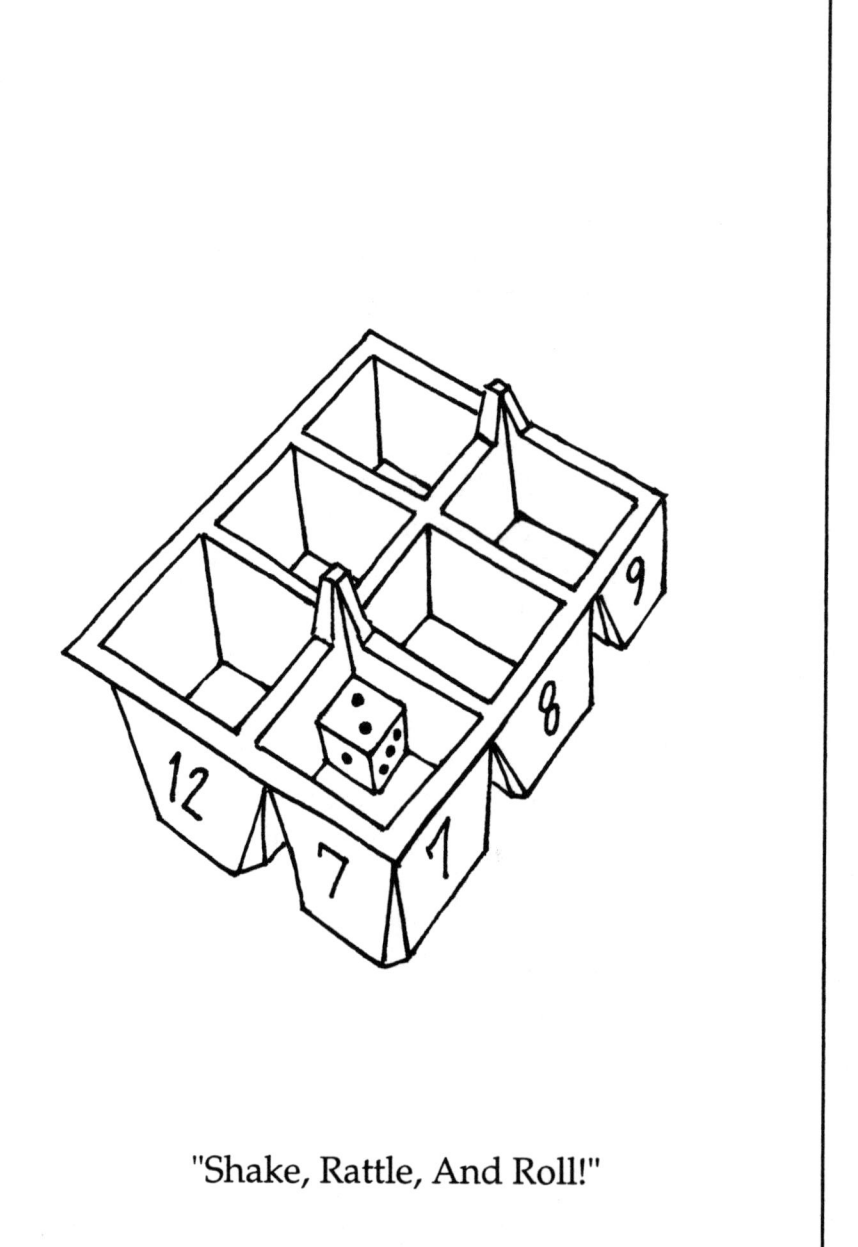

"Shake, Rattle, And Roll!"

"Shake, Rattle, And Roll!"

Objectives
To promote: ~ subtraction skills
~ visual perception
~ manipulative skills

Materials
* Six-cup egg carton
* Die
* Marker

Activity
Mark numerals 7 to 12 on cups of the egg carton. Place a die in the carton. Child will shake the carton. She will then subtract the number on the die from the number on the cup in which the die has landed.

154   *Subtracting Skills*

$$4 - 3 = 1$$

"Flash Cards"

"Flash Cards"

Objectives

To promote: ~ subtraction skills
~ observation skills
~ awareness of number usage in different contexts

Materials

* Deck of playing cards

Activity

Remove face cards and aces from deck and use playing cards like flash cards. Hold two cards up to the child. Child will subtract the lower number from the higher number.

156 *Subtracting Skills*

"Take Me Higher"

"Take Me Higher"
Activity for more than one child

Objectives
To promote: ~ subtraction skills
~ cooperation
~ task completion

Materials
* Deck of playing cards

Activity
Remove face cards from deck and have aces act as ones. Divide cards between two children. First child will turn over a card and place it on the table. If second child turns over a card which is lower, she will subtract the number of this card from the number of the higher card. If she turns over a card which is higher, the other player will subtract the numbers. Game continues until all the cards are used up.

158   *Subtracting Skills*

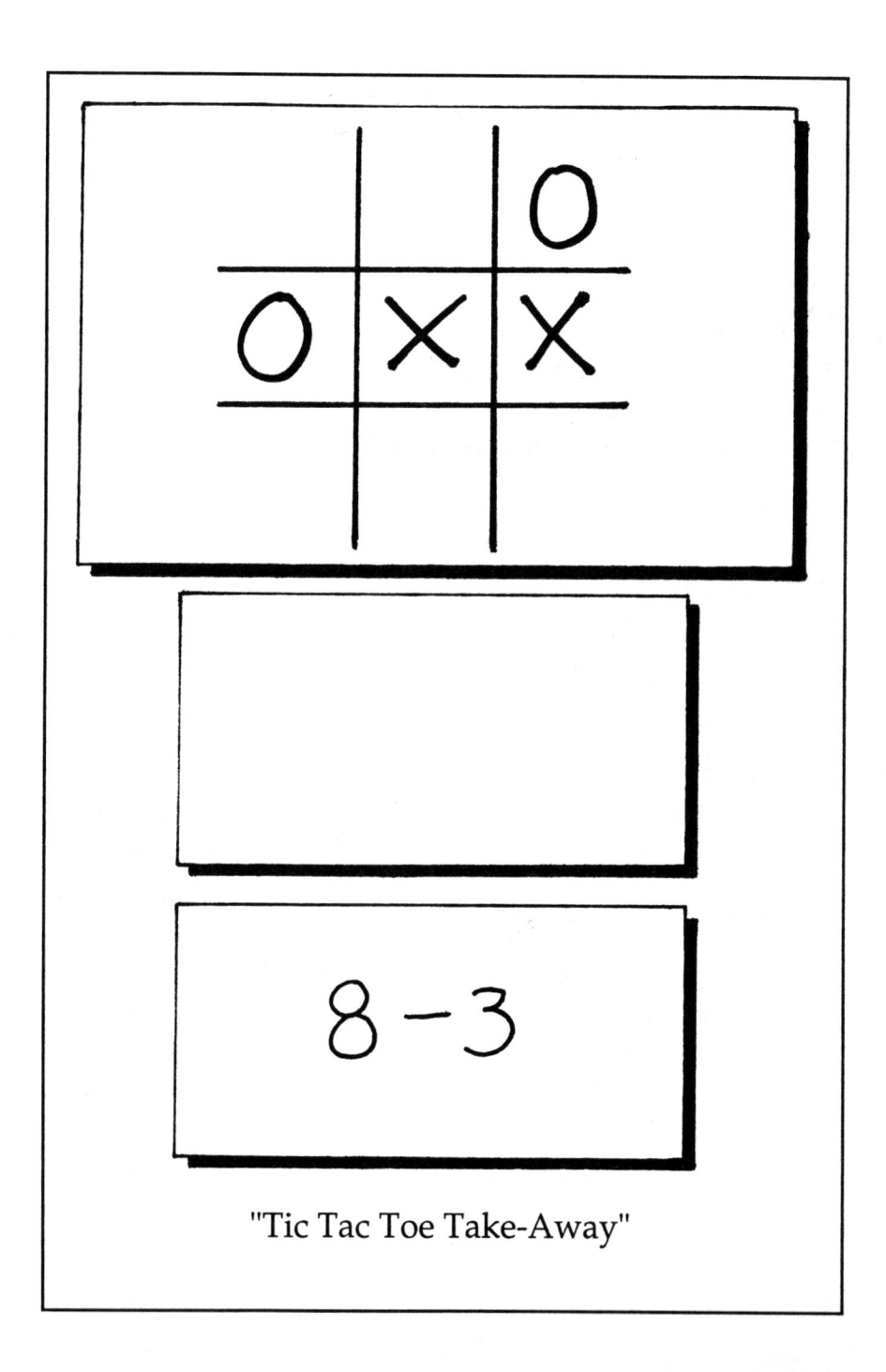

"Tic Tac Toe Take-Away"

"Tic Tac Toe Take-Away"
Activity for two children

Objectives
To promote: ~ subtraction skills
~ cooperation
~ development of small motor skills

Materials
* Index cards
* Paper
* Pencils

Activity
Write out subtraction problems on index cards and put them face down on table. Children will draw tic tac toe grid and then take turns picking cards and marking the grid with either an "X" or an "O" for every correct answer. Child will not mark the grid if her answer is incorrect.

160   *Subtracting Skills*

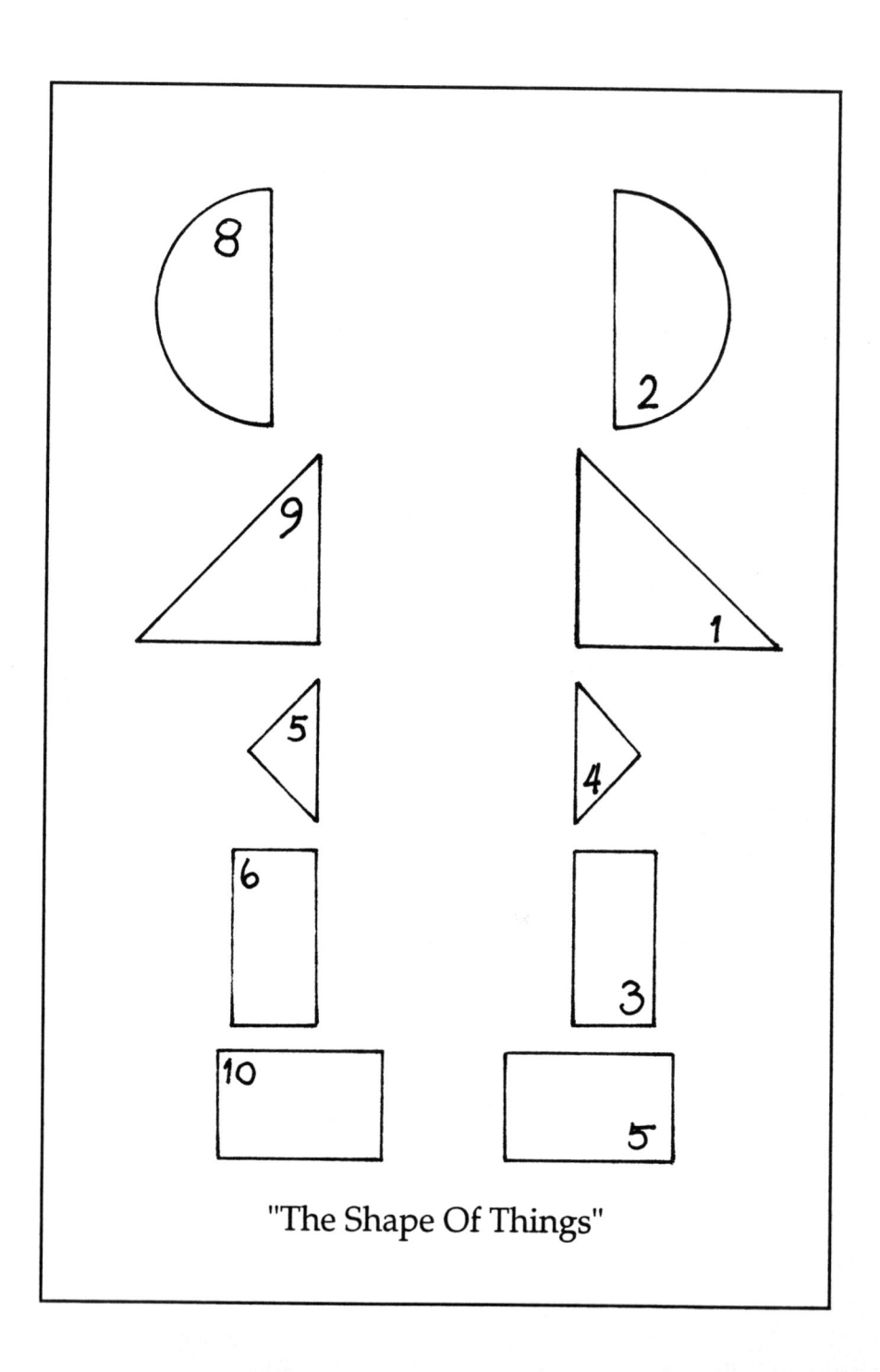

"The Shape Of Things"

"The Shape Of Things"

Objectives
To promote: ~ subtraction skills
~ shape recognition
~ development of small motor skills

Materials
* Construction paper
* Marker
* Scissors

Activity

From construction paper, cut out five different shapes. Write a numeral on the left hand side of each one, and a lower numeral on the right hand side. Cut them in half and give the half with the lower number to the child. She will match up the shapes and then subtract the lower numeral from the higher numeral for each one.

Section III

Using Money

Using Money

This chapter takes previously learned concepts; matching, sorting, classifying, adding, and subtracting, and applies them to the use of money. These activities help the child develop an understanding of the value of money and how it is used in every day life.

It should be noted that several of the activities in this chapter are far more complex than those in previous chapters and may require adult explanations and reinforcement. Use the activities judiciously and with supervision.

Recommended Materials

Assortment of coins & bills
Construction paper
Egg carton
Glue
Index cards
Jars or plastic containers
Markers
Newspaper
Plain paper
Pencil
Poster board
Sales circulars
Scissors

170 *Using Money*

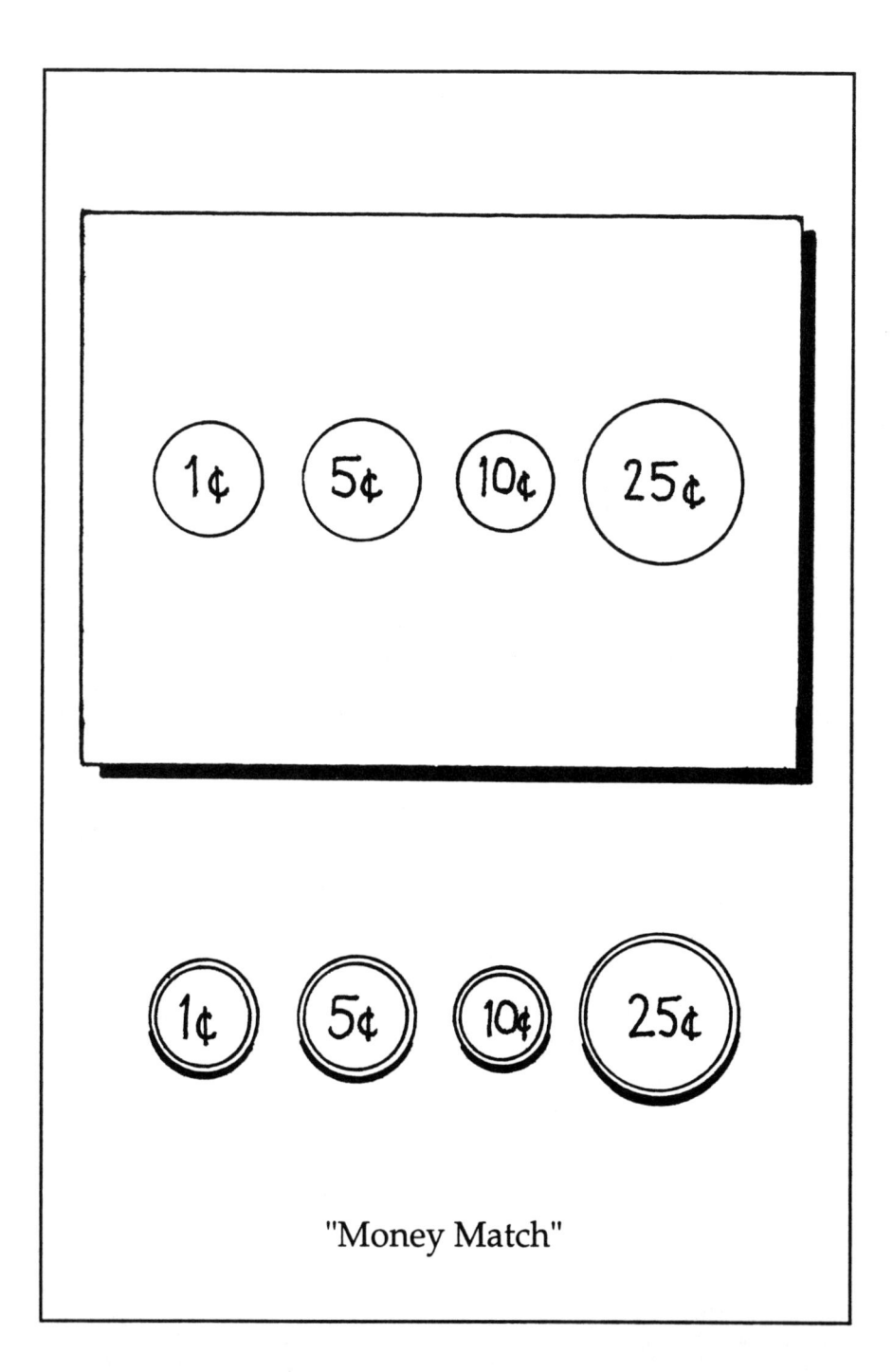

"Money Match"

"Money Match"

Objectives
To promote: ~ coin identification skills
~ matching skills
~ manipulative skills

Materials
* 5 x 8 index card
* Assortment of coins

Activity
On index card trace one penny, one nickel, one dime, and one quarter. Inside the circles write the corresponding amounts: "1c", "5c", "10c", "25c". Child will have an assortment of coins which she will correctly place on the circles.

172 *Using Money*

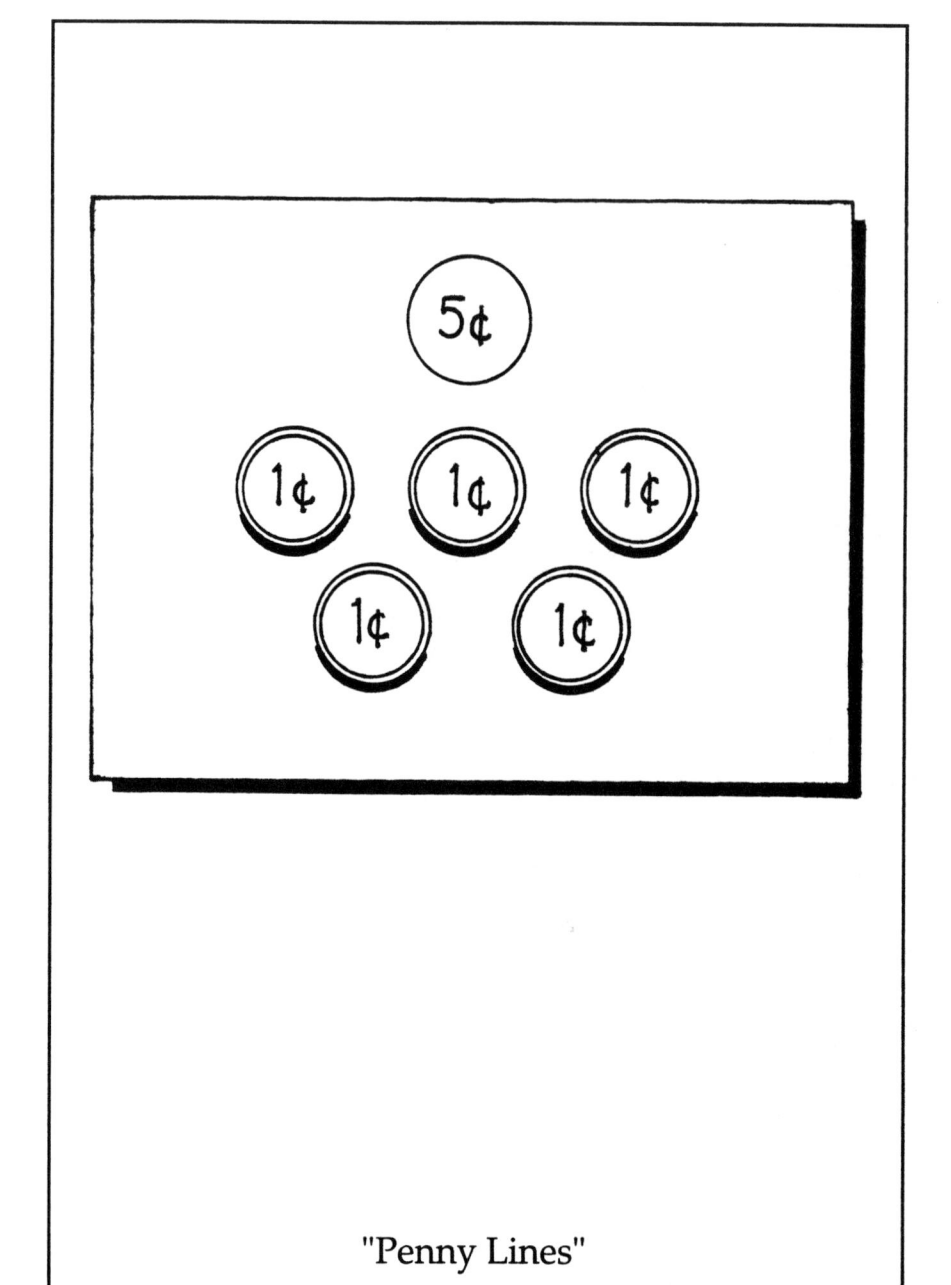

"Penny Lines"

"Penny Lines"

Objectives

To promote: ~ coin identification
~ counting skills
~ matching skills

Materials

* Four 3 x 5 index cards
* Forty-one pennies
* Markers

Activity

Trace a penny, nickel, dime, and quarter on separate index cards. Inside each circle write the amount it represents. Child will place the corresponding amount of pennies underneath the picture of each coin.

174 *Using Money*

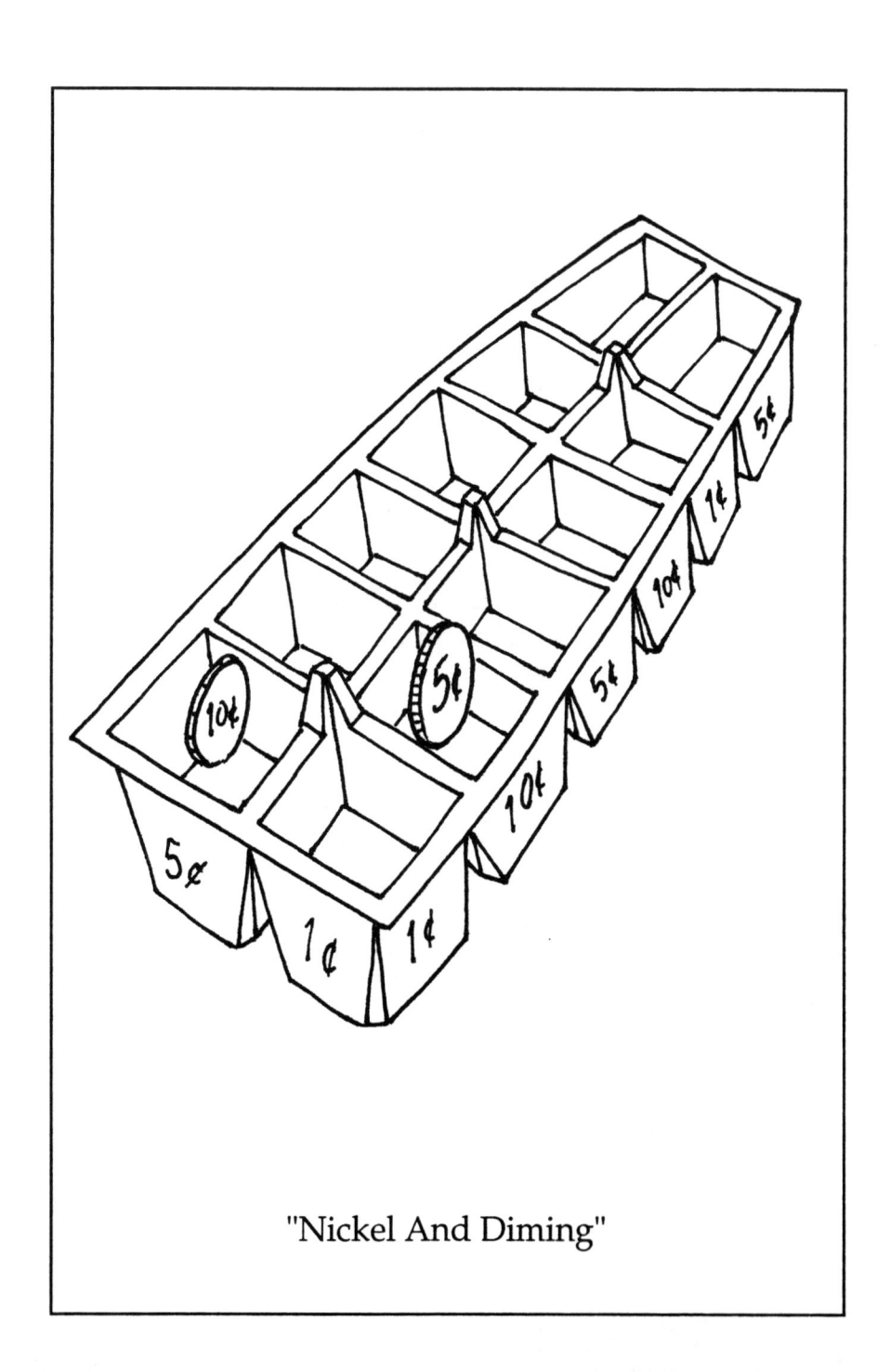

"Nickel And Diming"

"Nickel And Diming"

Objectives
To promote: ~ coin identification
~ addition skills
~ understanding of coin value

Materials
* Egg carton
* Nickel and dime
* Marker

Activity
Write different amounts of money in each cup of the egg carton. Place a nickel and a dime in the carton. Close carton and shake. Child will then add the value of each coin to the amount on the cup in which it has landed.

176 *Using Money*

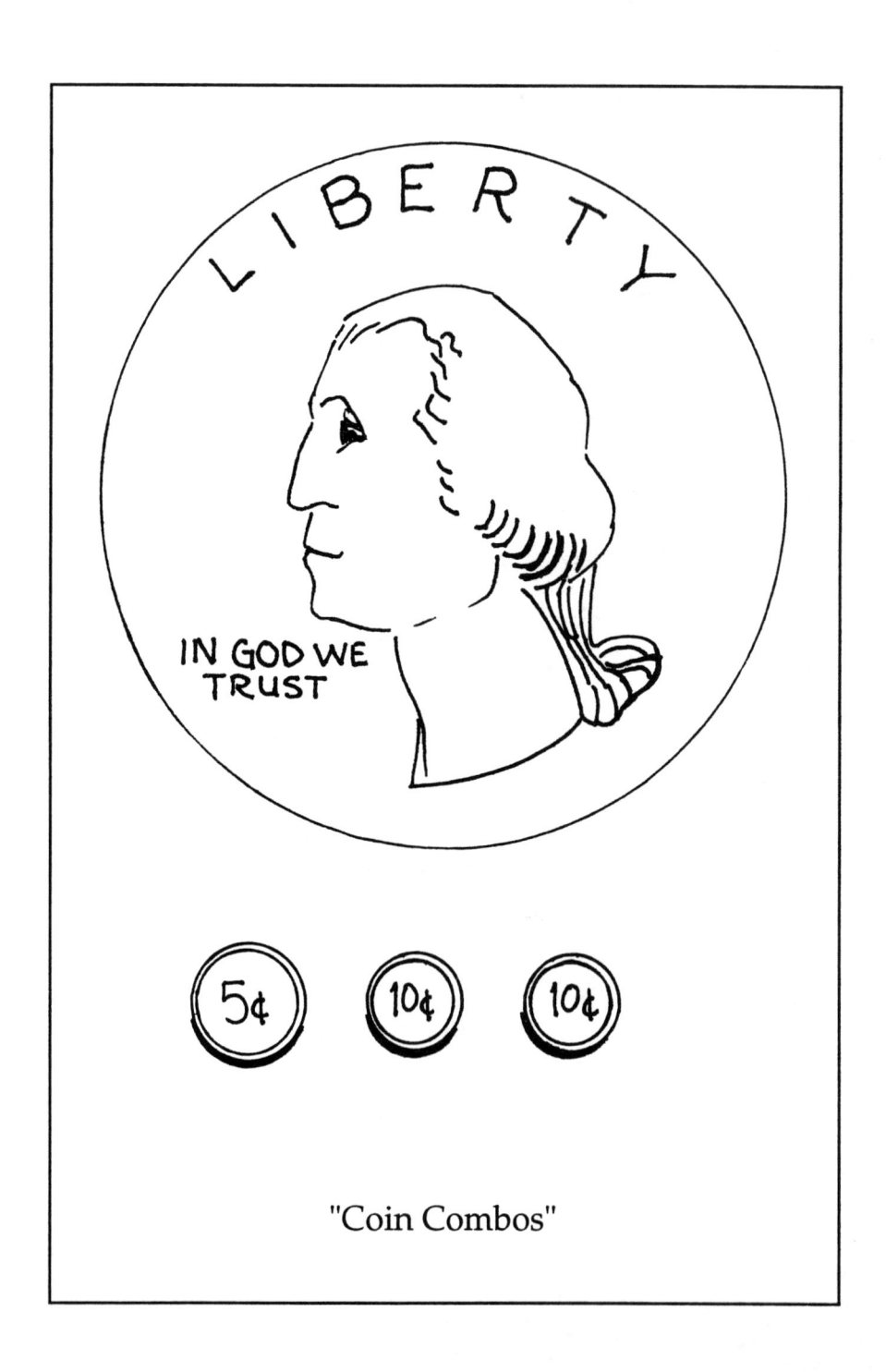

"Coin Combos"

"Coin Combos"

Objectives
To promote:
~ visual perception
~ understanding of coin value
~ use of different cognitive strategies

Materials
* Construction paper
* Assortment of coins
* Marker

Activity
Display a picture of a big "Quarter" coin. Child will use coins to find all the different combinations that make 25 cents. (Ex. 5 nickels; 2 dimes and a nickel).

178 *Using Money*

"Any Spare Change?"

"Any Spare Change?"

Objectives
To promote: ~ counting skills
~ understanding of coin value
~ development of small motor skills

Materials
* Five plastic containers or jars
* Assortment of coins

Activity
Mark each container with a different amount of money. Child will use coins to make corresponding amounts and then drop the correct amount of money into each container.

180   Using Money

"Bingo Bucks"

"Bingo Bucks"

Objectives

To promote: ~ coin recognition
~ addition skills
~ manipulative skills
~ understanding of coin value

Materials

* Construction paper
* Markers
* Assortment of coins

Activity

Mark squares on bingo board with different amounts of money. Give child an assortment of pennies, nickels, dimes, and quarters. When an amount (Ex. 30 cents) is called, child will cover the correct square with corresponding coins to make a total of 30 cents.

Shopping list

1 apple - 15¢

2 carrots - 20¢

1 lemon - 5¢

3 candies - 10¢

"Can You Loan Me A Dime?"

"Can You Loan Me A Dime?"

Objectives

To promote: ~ counting skills
~ word recognition
~ understanding of money usage

Materials

* Piggy bank (jar or plastic container can be used)
* Assortment of coins
* Construction paper
* Marker

Activity

Write out a list of food items with corresponding prices (Ex. 1 apple: 15c). Give child "piggy bank" filled with coins. Child will count the money in the piggy bank to see which of the items on the list she can buy.

184   Using Money

$2.96 ea.

$2.99 3L

$7.93

$45.80

ONLY $329.95

"Money, Money, Money"

"Money, Money, Money"

Objectives
To promote: ~ sequencing skills
~ money concepts
~ manipulative skills

Materials
* Newspaper
* Construction paper
* Scissors
* Glue

Activity
Child will find five different amounts of money printed in the newspaper. She will then stick them in correct order from the smallest amount to the largest.

186 *Using Money*

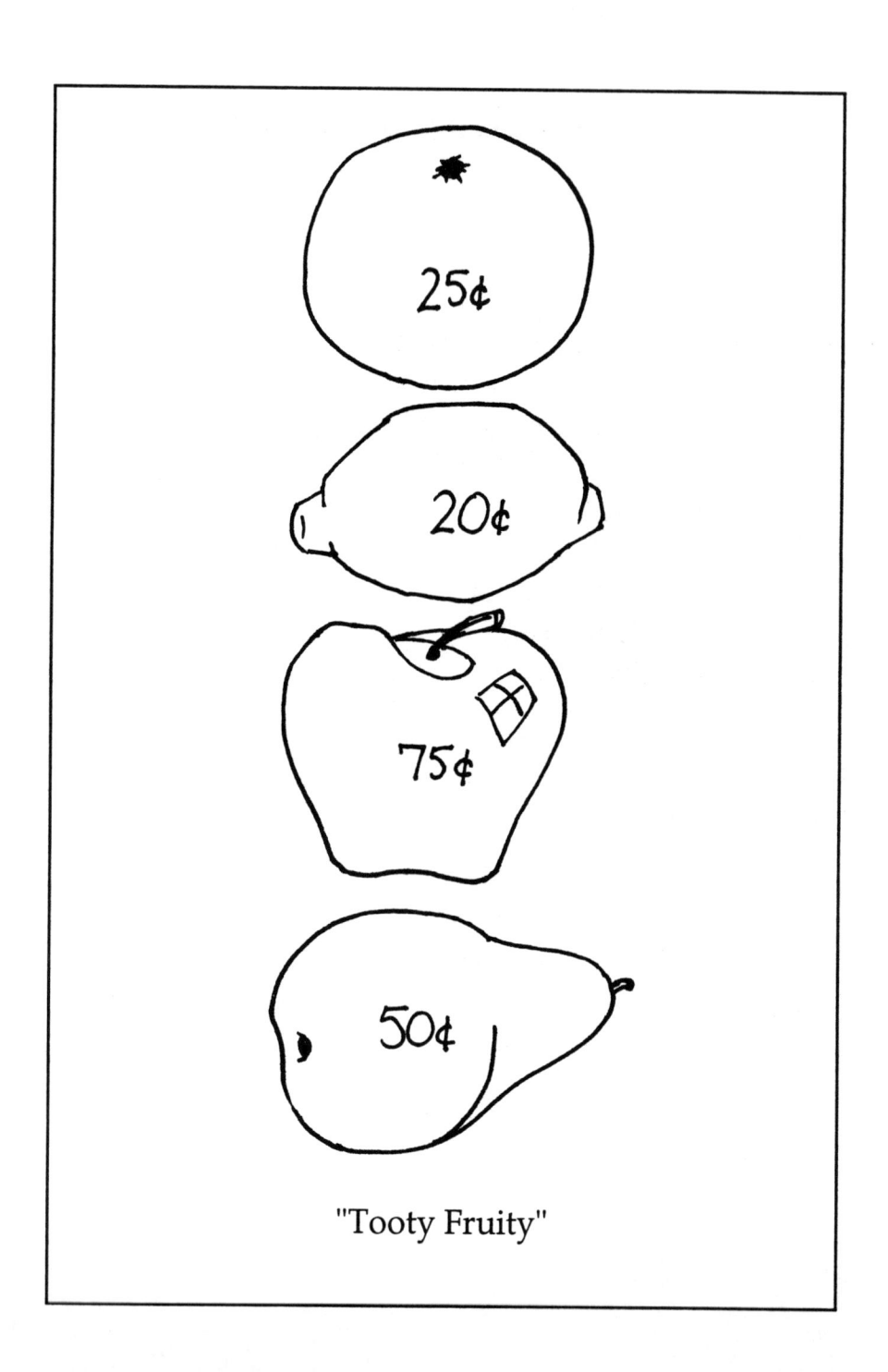

25¢

20¢

75¢

50¢

"Tooty Fruity"

"Tooty Fruity"

Objectives
To promote: ~ estimation skills
~ addition skills
~ information processing

Materials
* Poster board
* Scrap paper
* Different colored markers
* Pencil

Activity
On poster board, draw oranges, lemons, apples, and pears, and mark each type of fruit with a different price. Child will calculate which fruits she can buy with $2.

188   *Using Money*

Coupons	Retail Price
SAVE 40¢	$1.99
▮▮▮▮▮	$4.00
SAVE 35¢	$1.35
SAVE $1	$2.50
SAVE 50¢	$1.89
1/2 PRICE	$3.00

"Coupon Clippers"

"Coupon Clippers"

Objectives

To promote: ~ picture and word identification
~ subtraction skills
~ consumer education

Materials

* Sales circulars
* Sheet of paper
* Scissors
* Scrap paper
* Pencil

Activity

Cut out shopping coupons from sales circulars and write a list showing the retail price of each item. Give these to child. She will then calculate the price of each item using the discount shown on the coupon.

Using Money

PRODUCT OF U.S.A. RED RIPE AND JUICY
Fresh Cut Watermelon
1.30 per kg
.59 lb

PRODUCT OF U.S.A.
BAKE, BOIL OR MICROWAVE UNTIL TENDER
Fresh Yams
1.52 per kg
.69 lb

2 Litre
COCA-COLA CLASSIC, DIET COKE, DIET CAFFEINE FREE COKE, SPRITE, or DIET SPRITE
97¢ each
(4.85¢/100mL)

PRODUCT OF U.S.A. EXTRA FANCY GRADE
Granny Smith Apples
2.18 per kg
.99 lb

SELECTED VARIETIES
ASTRO YOGOURT
175g tub
.49

"The Price Is Right"

"The Price Is Right"

Objectives

To promote:
~ price recognition
~ visual perception
~ manipulative skills
~ addition and subtraction skills

Materials

* Sales circulars
* Scissors
* Scrap paper
* Pencil

Activity

Child will look through sales circulars and cut out five grocery items costing less than $1 each. She will then add up the total cost of items and calculate how much change she would have if she bought them with a $5 bill.

192   Using Money

269⁹⁸	$270.⁰⁰
89¢ pkg.	$1.⁰⁰
BONUS 19⁹⁹ VALUE	$20.⁰⁰
41 21	$41.⁰⁰
24⁸⁸	$25.⁰⁰

"Advertisement Amusement"

"Advertisement Amusement"

Objectives
To promote: ~ estimation skills
~ manipulative skills
~ consumer education

Material
* Newspaper
* Construction paper
* Scissors
* Pencil

Activity
Cut out a variety of sales advertisements from newspaper and stick them on a piece of construction paper. Child will round up prices from the ads to their nearest dollar and write the amount next to each one.

194 *Using Money*

```
         MENU
APPETIZERS      PRICES

Soup . . . . . . . . .50¢
Salads
      Chef. . . . . .75¢
      Garden...$1.00

Spinach Quiche..$1.50

Pizza Fingers...$1.00
```

"Guess Who's Coming To Dinner"

"Guess Who's Coming To Dinner"
Activity for more than one child

Objective
To promote: ~ word recognition
~ estimation skills
~ addition skills
~ understanding of money usage

Materials
* Colored paper
* Scissors
* Markers
* Assortment of coins (you can also use a $1 bill)

Activity
Create a menu showing the prices of different foods. One child will act as a server, and the other as a customer in a restaurant. The first child will pick items from the menu and pay for her meal with money, according to the prices listed. The other child will give back the appropriate amount of change. The roles can then be reversed.

*Telling
Time*

This final chapter introduces the relatively complex skills involved in telling time. Because of confusing terminology (Ex. quarter past, fifteen to, two "thirty", half of, 3:45, am, pm, etc.) and the differences between analog and digital time, it is suggested that adults provide a great deal of verbal explanation and emphasize the many different ways that time can be expressed.

These activities focus on the child's daily routines and should be modified and repeated often, using both analog and digital time.

Recommended Materials

Clock
Construction paper
Glue
Lozenge
Magazines
Markers
Newspapers
Plain paper
Paper fasteners
Paper plate
Pen
Pencil
Poster board
Scissors
Stop watch

202   *Telling Time*

"Clock Maker"

"Clock Maker"

Objectives

To promote:
~ time concepts
~ object replication skills
~ creative abilities
~ manipulative skills

Materials

* Paper plate
* Construction paper
* Scissors
* Markers
* Paper fasteners

Activity

Child will mark numbers of a clock face on a paper plate. From construction paper, she will then cut out a minute and hour hand and attach these to the clock face using paper fasteners. Clock can then be used to assist in calculating time in other activities.

"It's About Time"

"It's About Time"

Objectives
To promote: ~ time concepts
~ visual perception
~ individual choice
~ logical thinking

Materials
* Poster board
* Pictures of people in different daily activities (can be cut out of magazines and newspapers)
* Glue

Activity
Display pictures of people in different daily activities such as eating, shopping, reading, and sleeping. Child will estimate the time that these activities could be taking place. Clocks may be used as aids.

206   *Telling Time*

The time is . . .   The time is . . .

The time is . . .   The time is . . .

The time is . . .   The time is . . .

"Tic Toc... Tic Toc"

"Tic Toc... Tic Toc"

Objectives
To promote: ~ time recognition
~ reading skills
~ writing skills

Materials
* Construction paper
* Marker
* Pencil

Activity

On construction paper, draw clock faces showing different times. Underneath each face, write the sentence: "The time is...". Child will correctly complete the sentence for each of the times shown.

208   Telling Time

It is twelve o'clock

It is fifteen minutes after nine

It is fifteen minutes past six

"Time And Time Again"

"Time And Time Again"

Objectives
To promote: ~ time concepts
~ word recognition
~ understanding of written and digital time

Materials
* Poster board
* Construction paper
* Marker
* Scissors
* Glue

Activity

On poster board, write out a list of times (Ex. "It is twelve o'clock", "It is fifteen minutes after nine"). Cut out clock faces showing each of these times. Child will stick the clock faces next to the corresponding written times.

210 *Telling Time*

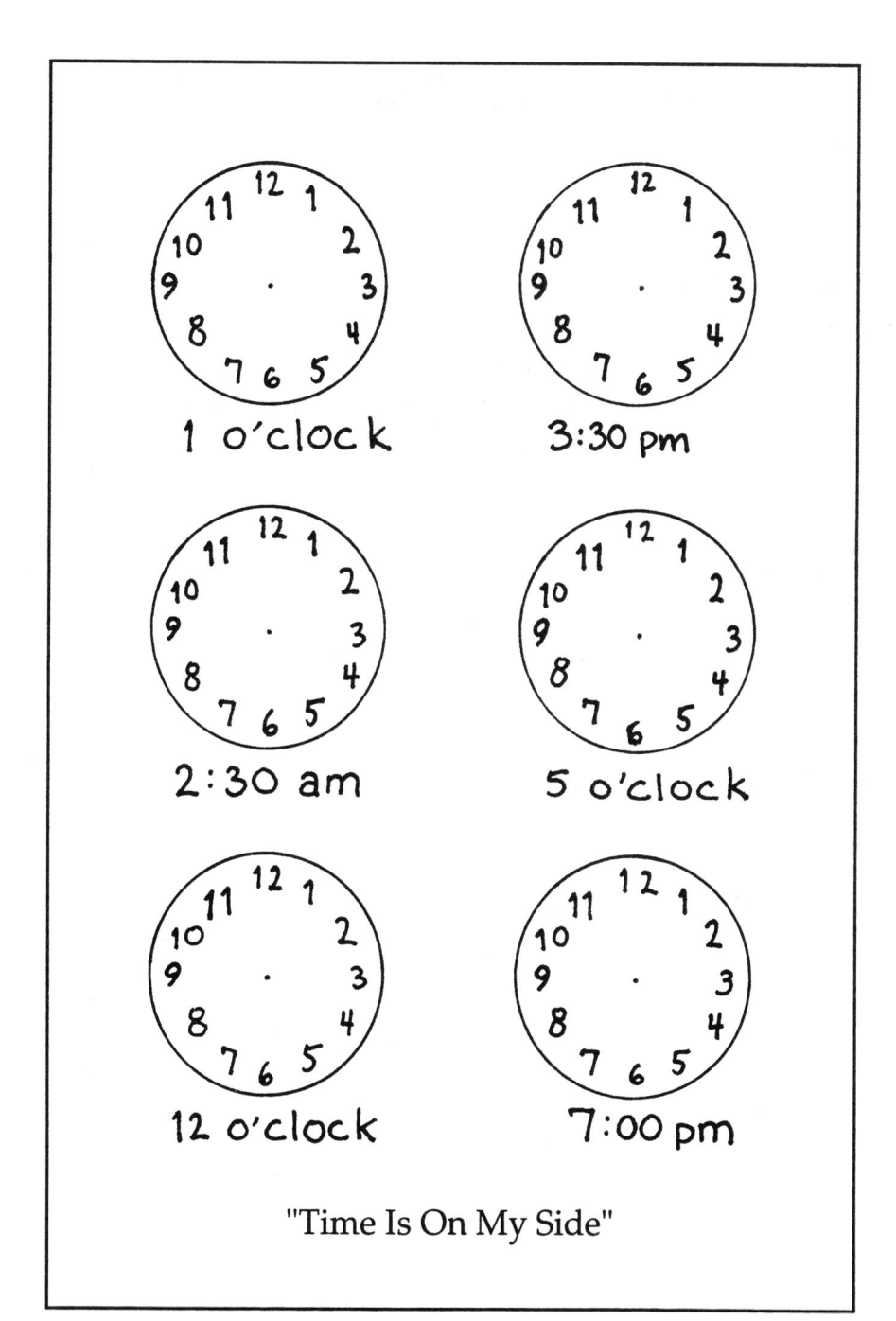

1 o'clock	3:30 pm
2:30 am	5 o'clock
12 o'clock	7:00 pm

"Time Is On My Side"

"Time Is On My Side"

Objectives
To promote: ~ time concepts
~ understanding of print words for time
~ manipulative skills

Materials
* Construction paper
* Sheet of paper
* Pen

Activity
On construction paper, draw clock faces showing numbers, but no hands. Underneath each face write a different time, Ex. "5 o'clock", "3:30pm", etc. Child will draw the correct hands on each of the clock faces to match the times shown.

212   *Telling Time*

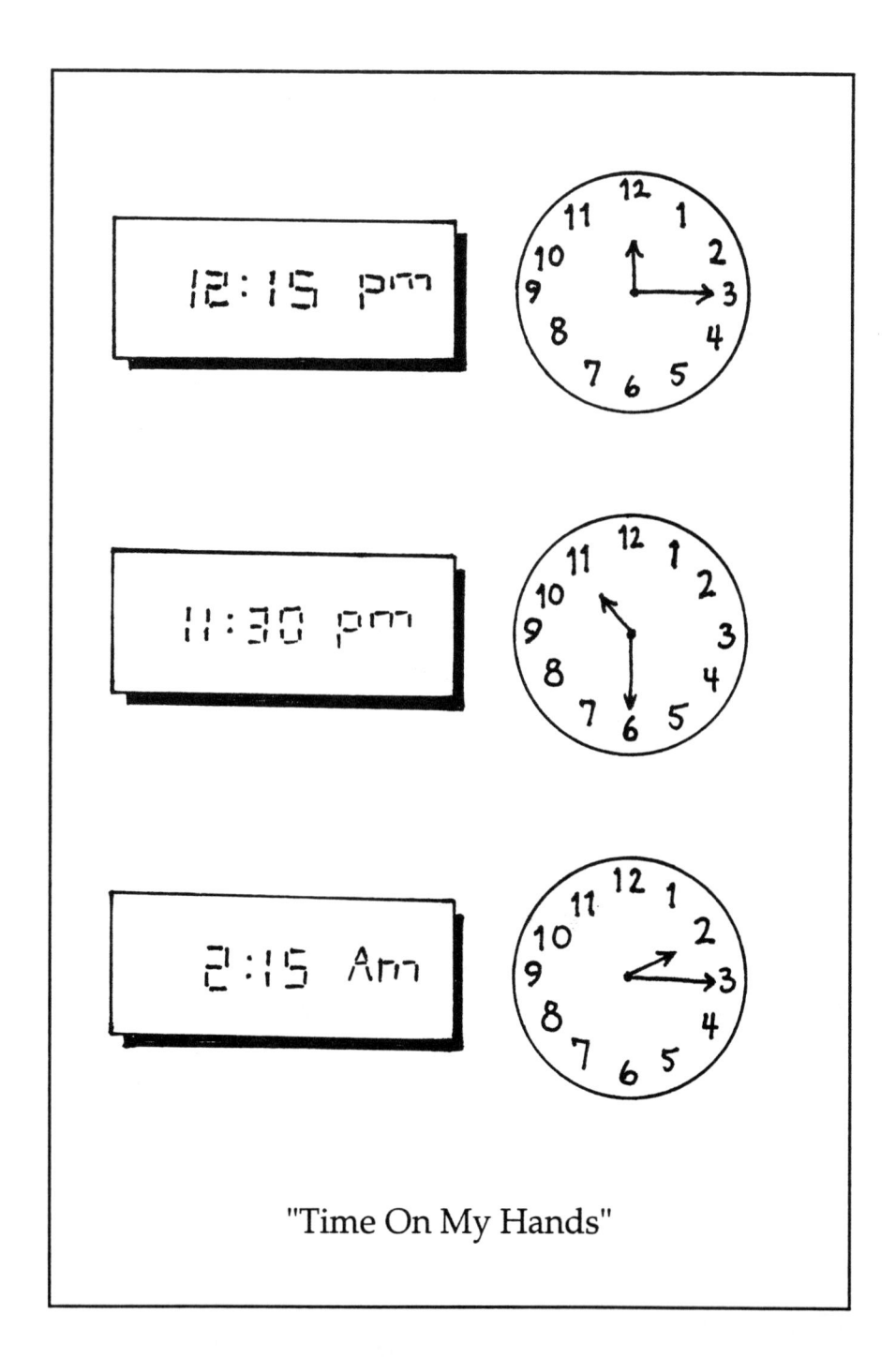

12:15 pm

11:30 pm

2:15 Am

"Time On My Hands"

"Time On My Hands"

Objectives
To promote: ~ matching skills
~ time recognition
~ understanding of analog and digital time

Materials
* Poster board
* Construction paper
* Marker
* Scissors
* Glue

Activity
On poster board, draw a row of clock faces, each showing a different time. Cut out corresponding digital times on separate pieces of paper. Child will stick the digital times underneath the matching clock faces.

214   *Telling Time*

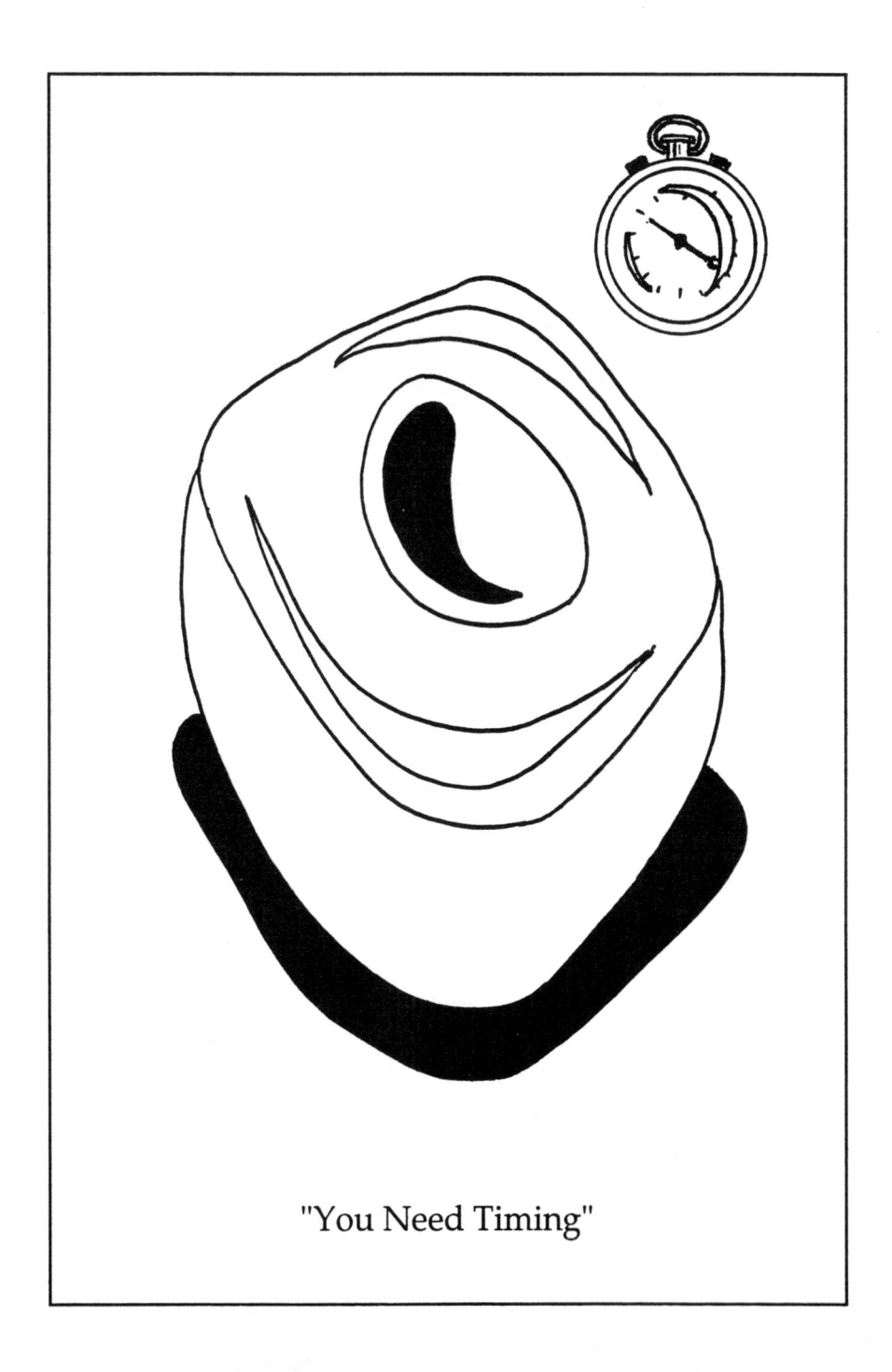

"You Need Timing"

"You Need Timing"

Objectives

To promote: ~ timing skills
~ understanding of time through different media
~ ability to compare differences

Materials

* One lozenge
* Stop watch
* Paper
* Pencil

Activity

Give child one lozenge. Using stopwatch, she will time how long it takes for the lozenge to dissolve in her mouth. This can be repeated with other foods and the times recorded and compared.

216 *Telling Time*

"The Time Is Right"

"The Time Is Right"

Objectives

To promote: ~ reinforcement of time concepts
~ visual perception
~ manipulative skills

Materials

* Poster board
* Construction paper
* Pictures of different daily activities (can be cut out of magazines or newspapers)
* Scissors   * Glue   * Marker

Activity

Stick pictures of different daily activities on poster board. (Ex. getting up, getting on school bus, going to bed, etc.) Cut clock faces out of construction paper and draw times on them to correspond with the activities. Child will stick the clock face showing the most appropriate time underneath each picture.

218   *Telling Time*

9:00 A.M.

10:00 am

10:30 AM

4:00 P.M.

6pm.

7:30 PM

"Where's The Time Gone?"

"Where's The Time Gone?"

Objectives
To promote: ~ time concepts
~ sequencing skills
~ manipulative skills

Materials
* Newspapers
* Sheet of paper
* Scissors
* Glue

Activity
Child will find five different times of the day printed in the newspaper. She will then cut them out and glue them in sequence from earliest to latest.

220 *Telling Time*

It is 3 o'clock when you leave school. It takes you fifteen minutes to walk home. What time do you arrive home?

"The Time Has Come"

"The Time Has Come"

Objectives
To promote: ~ understanding of time
~ estimation skills
~ logical thinking

Materials
* Sheet of paper
* Pen
* Clock (clock face made in first activity can be used)

Activity
Write a list of time problems for child. (Ex. "It is 3 o'clock when you leave school. It takes you fifteen minutes to walk home. What time do you arrive home?") Child will use clock to assist her and will write the correct time underneath each question.

222 Telling Time

12 o'clock

2:30 pm

"In The Nick Of Time"